SUSSEX
of
MIRTH *and* MAYHEM

Tony Wales

COUNTRYSIDE BOOKS

NEWBURY, BERKSHIRE

CONTENTS

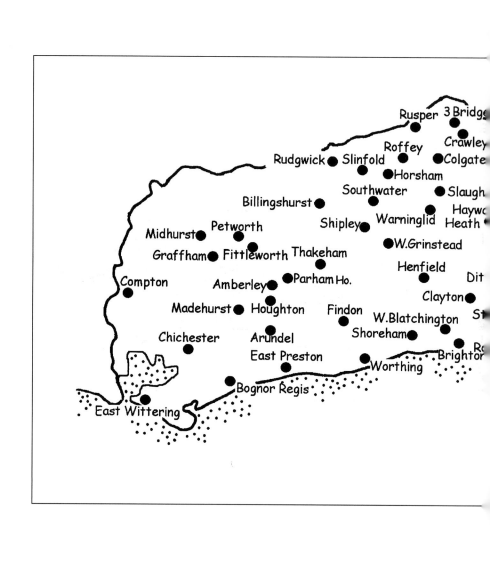

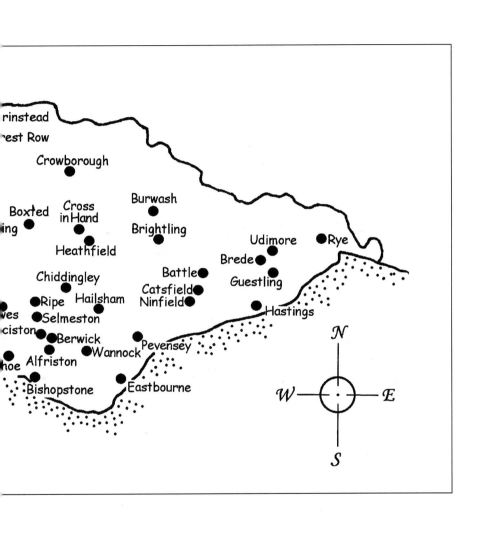

INTRODUCTION

Has the Sussex countryman (or woman) a strong sense of humour? My answer would be a positive yes. Sometimes the humour tends to be hidden from the onlooker, at least until we discover the unexpected sting in the tail. However, when we are dealing with the past, it is important to remember that life was not always funny – in fact often it was decidedly grim – so some humour can be a little caustic.

Townsfolk sometimes dismiss country jokes as coarse and crude, which attitude can be summed up in the phrase 'Strong in the arm and weak in the head', although in most cases this can be very inappropriate. However, it must be admitted that a few of our country 'characters' and 'eccentrics' may have contributed to this conclusion!

Perhaps typical Sussex country humour can be best illustrated by some examples. Sussex folk are notorious for their stubborn nature ('You may push and you may shuv, but I'm hemmed if I'll be druv'). For instance, the bell ringers of Burwash refused to ring the church bells in honour of King George IV because he had omitted to order their customary beer on a previous visit. And a young boy when admonished for staying away from school, replied with, 'Gooin' this sarfnoon, verlike'.

Obviously younger members of the community grew up with this obstinate streak. A boy of eight was told to avoid answering, when asked a direct question. When his retort to a simple query was, 'I dunno', he followed this up with the even more direct statement, 'Ye can't get over that, can ye?'

But some of the best examples of Sussex humour were probably well thought out, although they appeared at the time to be completely 'off the cuff'. When a man was asked how his family took their weekly bath, he replied that the water was heated in the kitchen copper, and then used in turn by all the members of the household. But he added that he drew the line at bathing in the water used by his mother-in-law. When the handle of a broom came off many times, the sweeper was heard to mutter, 'This danged handle has come off at least twenty times, and now to make things worse the head's come off.' A horse surprised its owner by falling down dead in the street. His astonishment was expressed by the remark, 'Well, I never knowed 'im play that trick afore.'

It was quite normal to be rude about other villages. The folk of one place would express their feelings about the people of the next village by a remark such as 'When they want to make a cart, they make a wagon and saw it in half'. Or 'When they want to make their church steeple higher, they pile manure around the base' (only they didn't actually use the word 'manure'). It was also possible to be rude to people in the same village – for instance, 'All her flannel petticoats are made of silk'. But your own village collected compliments such as 'It's got houses on both sides of the street'. Speaking of a large town such as London, then this could be described as 'Like the bustlin' part of Ditchling'.

Family jokes were highly prized, and retold many times. Such as how in my mother's family, father collected all the scraps from everyone's plate after a meal, intending them for the dog, but was carried away by the table conversation, and proceeded to eat them himself with apparent enjoyment. Meanwhile the youngsters held their breath until he had finished up the final morsel.

Many older Sussex writers were very attached to Sussex humour, including the Rev. John Coker Egerton in his lovely book *Sussex Folk and Sussex Ways* (1892). Here is one example quoted by him: A 'Heffle' (Heathfield) man was always in debt. He was noted as a late riser, and one day a neighbour insisted that his wife rouse him in order to settle a long outstanding debt. She failed in her endeavours, and later said sharply, 'Really, John. How can you lie sleeping when you owe all the money that you do?' His reply was, 'Oh, I can sleep very well. But I sometimes wonder how they can sleep that I owe the money to.'

Another fine Sussex author was the Rev. Edward Boys Ellman, who included much Sussex humour in his *Recollections of a Sussex Parson* (1912). Editor of the much lamented *Sussex County Magazine*, Arthur Beckett was also fascinated by his county's humour although he was sometimes irritated by it, particularly when it took the form of practical jokes, which were not to his taste.

I hope this little book will convince the reader (if this is necessary) that the Sussex countryman of old was by no means dull. Humour in daily life was often more important than is sometimes supposed, and a good joke was made to last a long time, and was handed around to be appreciated by as many as possible.

Sussex people are considered to be descendants of the Saxons, who rejoiced in the practical joke. They nicknamed the county Saelig Sussex, meaning, not 'silly' as is sometimes supposed, but 'happy' or 'blessed'. So you can see that Sussex folk have always found things to make them laugh.

Tony Wales

ACKNOWLEDGEMENTS

I am grateful to the following who have helped me compile this collection of Sussex humour. Some of these good people are no longer with us, but their names are included as a small mark of respect to their memory.

Bel Bailey; F. Barton; George Belton; Mabs Bryant; Agnes Childs; C.W. Cramp; Basil Evershed; John Fry; Arthur Garner; Nancy Godsmark; Gordon Hall; Frank Holmes; Jack Johnson; Peter Mackman; Sid Neve; Mr Newnham; Mary Page; Stan Parsons; David Piggott; Ethel Powell; Frank Venn; Mrs Vincent; Bob Wickens; Gladys Winton; Faith Woods; Rupert Taylor, *The East Sussex Village Book*, 1986; Swinfen Warden and David Arscott, *People of Hidden Sussex*, 1985; W.J. Wootton, *Wootton's Wannock Gardens*, nd; plus various issues of the *Sussex County Magazine*, the *West Sussex Gazette*, the *Petworth Society Magazine*, the *Countryman* and *Downs Country*.

PARSONS, PRIESTS and PARISH CLERKS

Churchgoers liked their pastors to be individualists, and so they did not object to a little eccentricity. Working folk also liked to feel that the vicar was 'one of them' rather than a member of the 'gentry'. A sense of humour, even if a trifle odd, was a welcome attribute.

Many country clergymen became very much a part of the village they served, staying quietly put for many years. But there were notable exceptions – men who were outstanding in some respect, shining brightly and dazzling those around them.

Frank Tatchell was Vicar of Midhurst from 1906 to 1935. He was undoubtedly a many-sided eccentric, and also a great traveller, journeying around the world many times whilst he left his flock to await his return. His advice to would-be travellers was, 'If attack-ed, meet the charge with a thrust of your umbrella. If the attack is from a mob, hurt one of the crowd and hurt him quickly. The rest will gather round the injured man and you will be able to slip away'.

Views like this made him popular with some, but unpopular with others. But as his sermons rarely lasted more than three minutes, he could not be accused of becoming a bore. Like some other country clergymen, he was sometimes criticised for allowing his muddy boots to peep from under his vestments.

His notices were eagerly awaited by his fans – such as 'Tramps whose boots are done for, can obtain new ones here'. This caused consternation in the local shoe shop which had to supply them. A notice in his garden said, 'Please walk on the grass', and he placed a message in his Parish Magazine: 'Will the person who took a plant of *Saxifrage Valdensis* from the Vicar's garden, call for the companion plant *Saxifrage Sardica*'. In his will he left 'all my clothes and boots to the Superintendent of Police, so that he might give them to passing tramps'.

Scholarly interests did not preclude the enjoyment of a good joke. Villagers responded to learning in their pastors, always provided it was mixed with the human touch. A good example was W.D. Parish who wrote many books, including the famous *Dictionary of Sussex Dialect*.

Parish was the much loved Vicar of Selmeston, until his death in 1875. At that time Selmeston was always pronounced 'Simpson', and it was as Vicar of Simpson that he was always known. As curate he was a popular school inspector, and in 1866 he supervised the rebuilding of Selmeston church, marking each stone so that it could be reset in its proper place.

When Parish was asked to make a donation to the Clergy Widows fund, his sense of humour got the better of him, and he pointed out that he was already helping Society by remaining single.

In spite of his many attributes, he lacked musical appreciation. When working in the library of Chichester Cathedral one day, he was irritated by the organ, which he thought was being tuned. When he asked the verger if the tuner could stop for a time, he was sternly informed that an organ recital was taking place.

Although unmarried he received a bill one day for repairing 'Mrs Parish's sealskin jacket'. Instead of explaining, he wrote back saying that Mrs Parish did not own a sealskin jacket.

One day when acting as inspector of schools, a tiny girl was overwhelmed by the occasion and burst into tears, whereupon he took her on his knee and allowed her to give him a kiss.

Many Parish Clerk stories are concerned with smuggling, when both the parsons and the clerks were implicated. However, sometimes the vicars were not included in the plot, and great pains were taken to try and keep them in the dark about the less than legal activities going on under their noses.

Hove and Preston were once served by one clergyman, on alternate Sundays. When due at Hove, the vicar arrived only to find that no preparations had been made. When he enquired the reason, he was politely informed, 'This is Preston Sunday, sir'. 'No, you are wrong. I preached there last Sunday.' The clerk persisted, and the vicar remained firm. Finally the clerk, completely exasperated, said, 'You can't preach here today. The church is full of tubs, and the pulpit is full of tea'.

Some priests and pastors were given nicknames. Father Bernard Cassidy (Horsham 1909–1941) was known affectionately as 'Cass'. He had a tremendous sense of fun, and he liked to shock those of his flock who he considered to be too strait-laced.

He had a number of unusual attributes, although he was less happy with children and I remember him as a rather frightening figure, who made me attempt to merge into invisibility whenever he spoke to me. At the same time I was fascinated by him and the astonishing things he accomplished in his church and parish, such as a marvellous Christmas crib with masses of small details, including even a figure of himself trudging towards the stable scene.

'Cass' hated noise, and when he was asked why he had built his presbytery walls so high, he replied it was to help people mind their own business.

One day a mouse ran up the cassock of the altar server, and the boy disappeared for a few moments in order to dispose of it quietly down in the cellar. Cass enjoyed this sort of thing, and rewarded the boy later with half-a-crown.

Father Bernard Cassidy – 'Cass'. He once walked a burglar to the police station.

Next door to the church grounds was an ironmonger's shop. Apparently Cass owed them fourteen shillings and ninepence, and the debt dragged on for some time. When pressed for payment, he appeared in the shop and emptied a sackful of farthings on to the counter (presumably from his Sunday collections).

When the presbytery was visited by a burglar, the priest gave him a long lecture, followed by a drink – and then walked him to the police station.

Some of the most successful village pastors were more popular with their village flock, than with their ecclesiastical superiors. What an interesting time the villagers at Thakeham must have had during the 19th century, when Parson John Hurst presided at their village church.

One day the numbers in Thakeham church were so few that Parson Hurst told the clerk to go next door and count the people in the local pub. As there were more than in the church, he decided to take his meagre congregation with him into the pub.

For some reason he fell out of favour with his superiors, and was not allowed to take services for a time. When he was permitted to return, he dressed up in his best vestments, and paraded through the village shouting, 'Here I am, back in harness'.

Like several others, he was a hunting-parson. One day he dismounted and urged his mount to go through a hedge whilst he hung on to the animal's tail, rather than be late for a service. His sexton kept a donkey in the churchyard, and one day it entered the church during a service. Hurst stopped his sermon, and shouted, 'Take that donkey out – there are too many here already'. When his own horse died, he buried it in his garden, in full harness, declaring it to be the animal's 'uniform'.

Next, a parson who seemed determined to upset as many of his congregation as he could, particularly if they were members of the 'upper class'. The Rev Edward Fitzgerald Synnot of Rusper wrote and published at his own expense a little book entitled *Five Years Hell in a Country Parish*. (This is now an extremely rare book, missing from most Sussex book collections – and if anyone can find me a copy, I will be very grateful!)

A parson who described his

women parishioners as 'the plainest lot I have ever seen' was unlikely to make friends among many of them, although strangely enough the Rev Synnot did have some supporters among his flock. But inevitably there were those, mainly the 'gentry', who failed to appreciate his particular brand of humour. He was criticised for singing too loudly, failing to chant in a melancholy voice, and marrying the wrong people. Among the latter were a 'lady of doubtful character', and a common 'roadster'. He said that his letters of complaint often included quotes from poets, which he claimed gave him a Course in the Classics.

When he was eventually summoned to a church court in London to explain many of his strange ways, he was exonerated and returned in triumph, to be met by his working-class fans and the Crawley Silver Band. This experience failed to shut him up, and he got back at his critics by preaching a sermon in which he spoke of his church clock being unlike many of his congregation 'as it was not two-faced'. When he left Rusper in 1932, this normally sleepy parish was content to lapse back into peace and quiet.

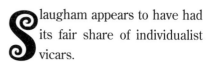

Slaugham appears to have had its fair share of individualist vicars.

One story occurs in *Memories of Slaugham*, which came to me in a manuscript written by V.H. Kensett in 1929.

Canon Ellison of Slaugham was very fond of standing in front of the kitchen fire on a Sunday morning. This led to the cooks getting into trouble 'upstairs' for the dinner being delayed. A new cook decided to put a stop to the problem, and when the Canon next stood in his accustomed place, she leaned over him with a ladle of hot fat, 'accidentally' shooting it over his clerical trousers. Surprisingly, she kept her place, although the Canon left the kitchen alone henceforth.

Also from the same village is this story of the Rev W. Sergison, who was involved in a dispute about church pews around 1857. The Reverend solved his problem by suggesting to some of the local youths that they should burn one of the offending pews – giving them half a crown to keep the whole thing a secret. They enjoyed making a large fire, so that no trace of the wooden pew remained. It was only after the parson's death that the secret leaked out.

Arthur Beckett was in his day one of the most popular writers on the lighter side of Sussex social history. His works are full of fascinating anecdotes, which modern authors (myself included) are very prone to draw upon. His *Adventures of a Quiet Man* (1933) has as a sub-title the following: 'A story with two heroes, a book of gossip and gossips, of country delights, of men, women and a dog, with extracts from a Commonplace Book and the Journal of the undersigned'. So if that doesn't make you want to read on, I cannot imagine what would.

In one of his books Arthur Beckett took great joy in writing about Parson Whistler, of Hastings, who he described as a 'humorist and an eccentric'. Bursting into a local shop one day, Whistler cried out, 'I have just tied a woman to a rock'. 'What made you do that?' was the astonished response. 'Because she wanted me to', was his answer. (He had in fact just married her to a man named Rock.)

One day the belfry of All Saints' church was being whitewashed. The painter accompanied the strokes of his brush by whistling a lively dance tune. When the vicar enquired if that was a suitable tune for a sacred place, the reply was, 'Beg pardon, sir. I forgot where I was'. Whereupon he changed to a slow version of the Old Hundredth, marking time with his brush. Quickly the parson shouted, 'Get back to your dance tune or the job will never be done'.

Some village parsons enjoyed 'a good day's sport' in the days when hunting was not frowned upon, although one can only wonder what effect this had on the carrying out of their day to day duties. But their congregation appeared to view this sort of behaviour as perfectly normal.

Parson Campion was one of the hunting clergy, and one day when following the hounds he landed in a ditch. Doctor Buddington was called for by some of the other riders: 'Here doctor, come back – the parson's in the Dick'. His reply was, 'Oh never mind he, we shan't want him till Sunday'.

Humour connected with the clergy was frequently deliberate and contrived, but as far as Parish Clerks were concerned it was more often completely unintended. The clerks were usually relatively uneducated men who desired a position of some slight importance, so they tried hard to maintain a dignified and serious mien – often with unfortunate results.

Arthur Beckett in one of his entertaining books mentions the clerk who wishing to make an important announcement in the local market, managed it in this fashion.

'Oyez, Oyez. This is to give notice that Good Friday, coming on Friday, the market will be postponed to the day before'.

Parish clerks sometimes despaired of the demands made upon them in order to sort out the actions of slightly muddled clergymen. Often relatively uneducated men, they had to make up in common-sense what they lacked in book learning.

When a country clergyman was searching for the book of Banns of Marriage, he was unable to find it in the usual place. Having started on the announcement, he kept on repeating, 'I publish the banns of marriage between. . . .' Until the clerk in a loud whisper helped him out with the message, 'Between the cushion and the desk, sir', which the parson repeated, much to the amazement of the congregation.

The announcements of parish clerks were not always exactly as planned. Mark Antony Lower wrote in 1845, that a few years earlier, a gale had unroofed several barns, blowing down a windmill.

It was just at the time for the psalm before the sermon, and the clerk rose and astonished the congregation with the words, 'Let us sing to the praise and glory of . . . please sir, Mus' Cinderby's mill is blowed down'.

Michael Turner of
Warnham. A local dandy,
and strict choirmaster.
Boys who tried any
mischief were flicked with
his fiddle bow.

Clerks often had to cope not only with difficult priests, but also with the vagaries of village church choirs.

On one occasion the parish clerk played the tune of the hymn he had chosen, expecting the choir to follow. However, this was not the tune they wanted, so dead silence ensued. The clerk, who was not used to having his wishes ignored, stood at the foot of the gallery and shouted up to them, 'Be ye agoin' to sing today, or baint ye? Becus' if ye baint agoin' to sing, then I baint agoin' to play.'

Sometimes it was the clergyman who was sorely tried by the actions of his clerk. One wet Sunday the clergyman of a Downland church fell from his horse, and his clothes were saturated. He told the clerk to announce to the congregation that because of a slight accident, he would be unable to preach. After prayers, the clerk rose and said, 'Ye-be to goo now, Passon ant a-gooin' to praich to-dey acause he's wet 'is-self'.

One more similar parish clerk story. A Sussex sporting parson wished to attend the races at Worthing on Monday. In order to be on time, he told his clerk that the usual Sunday afternoon service would not be held. The clerk horrified him by giving out, 'This is to give notice that there won't be no sarvise this arternoon, 'cos parson be agwine to Worthing to be in time for the races'.

In 1946 Edmund Austen wrote an entertaining book *Brede – the story of a Sussex Parish'*. Among the mass of memories and local history, he included several items of humour and dialect, including this story of a Brede wedding.

The clerk asked the bride and groom, 'What do you want? A tinkle or a blast?' When asked what was the difference, they were told: 'A tinkle – that's me, the missis and de boy – and dat'll be a shilling. But if you want a blast – dat'll be all de lot an' us, and dat'll be thirty shilling'.

They chose the 'blast', and were well satisfied.

In to musicians and singers, and we are left with the firm impression that if clerks and parsons could be difficult, then musicians could beat them any day.

This is the much-quoted story of the irascible old man who, putting great energy into his playing of a favourite hymn tune, caused his fiddle string to snap. In fury he flung the offending instrument down from the gallery into the church, shouting, 'Goo down there, and bide there', and what's more he refused to play again.

Sometimes it was the whole choir who fell out with the vicar, as once happened at Amberley.

In fact the whole lot went on strike, and in retaliation the vicar persuaded the pub landlord to 'freeze his taps' against them. They responded by whitewashing his windows during the night, and giving him 'Rough Music' during the day.

K.H. MacDermott in his *Sussex Church Music in the Past* (1922) wrote most entertainingly about Sussex choirs and musicians. There was, for instance, the man who came to Selmeston Vicarage and began singing a Christmas carol, all by himself. He felt it necessary to explain his solitude, and wished to get on with the hymn at the same time. So this is how it went.

'While shepherds watched their flocks by night (if you please sir, my party's all jacked up) All seated on the ground (There was young Harry down here) The angel of the Lord came down (And my brother Jem and Tom and George, we've all bin practisin' together) And glory shone around (but nary one on'em would come wi' me, they've all properly jacked up, sir!)'.

When church bands went out of fashion, the new fangled barrel organs appeared. These were much to the liking of the Sussex countryman with a sense of humour, and soon the most unlikely tales began to appear concerning these instruments. No doubt many are of doubtful authenticity, but are worth repeating.

Berwick barrel organ was worked by clockwork. One Sunday it gave a click at the end of a psalm and proceeded to play *Little Drops of Brandy*, followed quickly by *Go to the Devil and Wash Yourself*.

At Stanmer the new barrel organ would not stop playing. In desperation the clerk threw it into an open grave outside the church. Here it carried on with *All People that on Earth do Dwell*.

Many of the barrel organs had secular as well as sacred tunes. In 1790 the machine used at Parham church included in its repertoire such choice items as *He's ay a'kissing me* and *With my mug in my hand*.

It has to be admitted that church bell ringers were often noted for their attachment to strong drink. At Slaugham the ringers had imbibed rather freely one night. Returning home about midnight, some of them found difficulty in managing a stile, and one particularly awkward character managed to get astride a donkey in a field, rather than the stile. Frightened he yelled out, 'Oh good De'il. Don't take me. I am a good bell ringer and not a wicked man'. The donkey was more frightened than the man, and took off across the field, whereupon the rider fell off.

Henry Burstow of Horsham was famous in his day as an expert ringer. He plied his art just for the joy of ringing, often in unfamiliar belfries. Several years ago I was able to find a few Horsham folk still around, who remembered old Henry and were able to recount many tales about him, and how he walked miles to join bell ringers in distant churches.

In his *Reminiscences* (1911) he told of an occasion when the Horsham ringers were due to start ringing the old year out at about 11.30. Something or other upset several of them and arguments broke out. Finally Ned Sturt and another of the men began tussling, pulling each other round the taproom of the Talbot. They had just broken a chair in the struggle, when Ned's wife appeared and seizing a leg of the broken chair she attacked the second man, saying, 'I'll teach you to interfere with my man – clear out'. And clear out they all did rather quickly, just in time to pull the bells before the clock struck twelve. Afterwards Ned Sturt was condemned by his wife to a sober life, and never came out ringing again.

And from a village churchyard in West Sussex, the following was noted.

Here lye the bones of Joseph Horton.
Whose death was curiously brought on.
Seeking one day his corn to mow off.
His razor slipped, and cut his toe off.
His toe, or rather where it grew to.
The inflammation quickly flew to.
And then it started mortifying,
And that was the cause of Joseph dying.

In spite of their rather grim occupation, grave diggers were not without a strong sense of humour. When one was asked how deep he dug his graves, he replied, 'Them as I don't like, I put down another two feet, so that they will be late for the resurrection.'

The following story came to me from Mr Laker of Three Bridges, who had a liking for tales of this kind. However, it must be said that similar tales exist from elsewhere.

One New Year's Eve, one of the village bloods decided to frighten the local grave diggers, so he dressed up in a long white nightdress and floured his face. When he appeared, one of the diggers enquired of another, 'Who do you rackon that is then?' The one addressed replied, 'I dunno, but it ain't one o' mine. I allus dig mine in praper'.

A weak-minded gentleman who sometimes helped the grave diggers, was asked to help with the grave of a man who had tormented him. When the job was done, he jumped on the grave, stamping down the earth and yelling, 'Got ye now. Got ye now.'

The Warnham sexton and gravedigger. A strange character to appear on a Christmas greetings card in 1905!

My old friend Sid Neve was always ready with some good stories of his early years, including this one about an undertaker who lived halfway between Ninfield and Catsfield.

Justice Hawkins was badly hen-pecked, although he always managed to give his wife the slip in order to visit the local pub. One Saturday night, having had one-over-the-eight, he staggered home and made his way to his primitive privy. A heavy man, he forgot that the seat had become somewhat infested with woodworm. With his sudden weight it disintegrated and Justice collapsed into the odoriferous bucket.

He could not summon the courage to go indoors, so he took shelter in the shed where he built his coffins. Stripping off his clothes, he spent the night in one of his wooden creations. At dawn his wife found he was missing from her side, so she went down to the shed to see if he had started work early. She found him lying naked in a

A typical back garden privy, similar to the one where Justice Hawkins had his mishap.

coffin, with an unearthly pallor. Thenceforth he was condemned to a single bed downstairs, and he found it expedient to sign the pledge.

A MISCELLANY of MILLERS

Perhaps a little unfairly, Sussex millers tended to enjoy a reputation for dishonesty and double dealing. It was said that the only way to tell an honest miller was to check whether he had a tuft of hair in the palm of his hand. However, when one man challenged a particular miller to show him his tuft, the reply was that only an honest man could see it.

There were many stories concerning millers which underlined this dishonest trait, although obviously no miller would ever agree that there was a grain of truth in any of them. A typical tale, repeated many times, went like this:

A villager met the local miller and asked if he could take his gleanings up to the mill to be ground. 'Why sure, but be certain to ask Tom to hang up the Old Black Cat.' Although not understanding this remark, he did as he was told. Whilst he waited for his grain, he noticed an extra sack hanging from a nail. 'So that's the Old Black Cat, is it?' he remarked. Quickly he picked up a scoop and took a couple of helpings of flour from a nearby bin, and added these to his own sack. On his way home he met the miller again, who asked if he had remembered to tell Tom about the Black Cat. 'Yes', was the reply. 'I told him, and I also had a couple of her kittens'.

Mark Anthony Lower, the Sussex historian, noted a rhyme on a mill, in 1854, evidently by an unknown miller. This ended with:

The motion of the mill is swift,
The miller must be very thrift.
To jump about and get things ready,
Or else the mill will soon run empty.

Hardly good poetry, but good sense nevertheless.

Apart from honesty, or the lack of it, millers seem to have been a particularly eccentric bunch. Perhaps it was the often solitary life they led that resulted in some very weird and singular traits. One such was Tom Hurst of Rectory Manor Mill at Eastbourne, who was particularly fond of a wager whenever the opportunity presented itself.

One pay day, Tom accepted a bet that he and his horse could carry a cartload of corn around the mill – a cartload being ten sacks each of two and a half hundredweight. Tom then took five of the sacks himself, and put the other five on the unfortunate horse. He won the wager, but the back of the horse was broken. In spite of his eccentricities, Tom was a kindly man, and he almost cried as he said, 'If I had thought it would have done for her, I would have managed another one myself.'

However, it was not only millers who inhabited the mills. When their working days were done, mills were sometimes used as homes for those with a taste for the unusual. Edward Martin wrote a book *Life in a Sussex Windmill* in 1921, in which he told of living in the Clayton mill 'Jack'.

Mr Martin found that he had to share his unusual home with many other creatures such as mice, slugs, earwigs and silver fish. A sense of humour was essential, in order to survive being peered at through his windows by both natives and visitors – the latter expecting him to be there to supply them with refreshments such as ginger beer and milk. One man even walked in uninvited and made himself at home. Because the walls sloped inwards, the pictures which Mr Martin wished to display on his walls, hung vertically and flapped around in the wind. When the door was open on a windy day, every loose object in the living room whirled around at will.

For real eccentricity we must turn to Miller Oliver of Highdown Mill, near Worthing. Born in 1709, he is remembered chiefly for having erected his own tomb, thirty years before his death. The tomb may still be seen, although I doubt if local children still run around it twelve times to encourage the Devil to appear – as Winifred Whiting told me they did in her childhood. It was also believed that Miller Oliver was buried upside down in his tomb, so that on Judgement Day when the world will be turned upside-down, he would be the only one the right way up. Not so far away, on Box Hill in Surrey, a Major Labelliere who died seven years after Oliver, was also supposedly buried in the same fashion, for a similar reason.

Highdown's eccentric miller not only erected his own tomb but he also made his own coffin which was fitted with castors, so that he could pull it out from under his bed. On it he was supposed to have inscribed:

> Beneath my bed, my coffin stands.
> On four wheels, swift it runs.
> I am always proud to show the same,
> And why my neighbours, do you me blame?

Miller Oliver's tomb at Highdown near Worthing. He was a true Sussex eccentric.

Another side to his character was that of a model-maker. One of these was of a Customs Officer chasing a smuggler, with an old woman following the latter with her broom. Not inappropriate, as he had a reputation as a smuggler, and it was said that he would arrange the sails of his mill in such a way as to signal to his smuggling associates when the coast was clear for them to land their contraband.

In the latter part of the 19th century, an old dame, Hannah White was to be seen regularly on Highdown Hill with a basket of home-made sweets, offering for a few pence to relate the story of John Oliver and his eccentricities.

The famous Sussex author and historian Hilaire Belloc purchased Shipley Mill in 1906. Belloc loved his mill, and christened it 'Mrs Shipley'. Although not really a Sussex man, he felt very much at home in the county, and was delighted when he heard that in answer to an enquiry, an innkeeper had replied that he did not know of a writer called Belloc, but he knew of a fellow of that name who farmed near Shipley.

On New Year's Eve, Belloc liked to parade his family outside the mill to hear the cannon being fired from Warnham Court at midnight. He was determined that first footing should be by a male, and he even made sure that his cat did not usurp this position.

Local folk viewed Belloc with affection, tinged with a little amusement. He was certain that the water he drank tasted better if it came from a certain well, some distance away. He employed a local boy to fetch the water each day, but the lad not being keen on such a long walk, brought the water from his grandmother's well a few steps away – leaving enough time so that the writer would not realise that the water he enjoyed so much, didn't actually come from the well of his choice.

My step-mother who lived as a child in the area, recalled how Belloc and his friend Chesterton used to attend the Roman Catholic church at West Grinstead, dressed in their long black cloaks, slightly spoilt by the bulges of the bottles they carried with them. But with all his eccentricities, Belloc was a delightful man, who wrote, 'When I am dead, I hope it may be said, His sins were scarlet, but his books were read'.

ocals, particularly the youngsters, were fascinated by the action of the mills. This often caused mishaps, although it failed to deter those who wished to gain amusement and entertainment from this monster in their midst. There are many tales of local dare-devils, not always the younger members of the village, who took their life in their hands for a bet, or even just for the sheer fun of it.

James Goble of Houghton was known as 'Lord Moon' in the 19th century, because of his habit of grabbing the vanes of the mill in order to be carried round with the sweeps. Once this ended with him being thrown over a 16 foot fence.

When townsfolk asked what the sails were for, the country wag replied, 'Why, for topping and tailing gooseberries, of course'. A country joke was to declare that two mills could not be erected close to each other, as there would be too little wind to operate both of them. Two famous mills together, at Clayton near Brighton, were known as 'Jack and Jill', making this remark superfluous!

One would expect locals to treat the familiar mills with little respect, but one old countryman who was taken to the top of the Clayton mill 'Jack', as a treat on his 70th birthday, was so dumbstruck by the view

Jack and Jill windmills at Clayton near Brighton. They feature in many good stories.

that he remarked, 'I never knew the world was so big'.

Sometimes a bit of fun could go very wrong. It would be expected that local tragedies would deter future mishaps, but this seldom seemed to be so. The mill at Cross-in-Hand built in 1806, was the setting for a wager between two labourers. One bet the other that he could not run between the sweeps as they rotated. The feat was accomplished, but in trying to repeat it, the man was struck and killed.

Not all tales were so tragic, and sometimes a large slice of local humour was provided by the mill.

When West Blatchington mill was due to be re-tarred, the job was taken on a by a man with a particularly shrewish wife. Swinging aloft in a cradle, he realised that he could be brave enough to taunt his wife, whilst she was unable to reach him. Soon she was in tears of frustration as she stood beneath him, and during the time it took him to tar the mill, local folk delighted in listening to the couple's cross-talk.

West Blatchington Mill at Hove.
Once part of a Sussex farm, but now
surrounded by modern buildings

A famous Sussex book is the *Dialect Dictionary* compiled by the Rev W. D. Parish and published originally in 1875. (It was later expanded by Helena Hall in 1957.) Although scholarly, it is also tremendously entertaining, and includes some lovely anecdotes concerning Sussex folk.

Old Mrs Wells of Lindfield had been away for a fortnight on a holiday. Being asked about it she said she had had a very pleasant time, but could not say where she had been staying. At last she said 'Well I know it were a shilling the other side of Lewes'.

A peasant at Ditchling reading aloud a notice of the death of a resident – The deceased (he pronounced this 'diseased') came to Ditchling about a decade (decayed) back. 'Ah' he said, 'I rac'n'd 'eed got summat a matter wid 'im, but I did'n allow 'twer 'is back'.

At Midhurst, a stranger asked 'Where is the bathing place in the river?' and was told cheerfully 'You goos thro' the 'ood till yer comes to the post put up where the butler was drowned an' that's it'.

And one more . . . 'E was Swish I think – leastways a German sort of genilman with spartacles as smelt o' smoke'.

Even in an age of eccentrics, Sussex mill lore abounds with 'characters' who provide us with some lovely stories. Featured in one tale was William Catt, who harnessed the power of the sea to grind corn in his Bishopstone Tide Mill. He was reputed to be a stern man, so much so that one of his men was reputed to have said to him, 'Gie us yer hand, sir – I love ye, I love ye, but I'm danged if I be'ant afraid of ye though.'

Lastly, a personal memory of the old steam mill in Denne Road, Horsham. As a very young boy I was fascinated by the metal model of a steam engine high up on the front of the mill building.

Later the model engine ended its days in Horsham Museum, and the curator wondered why the surface of the metal was pitted with tiny impressions. What he didn't know was that for years the engine had been a favourite target for local boys with their catapults.

SHOPKEEPERS and SHOWMEN

In the past, shops tended to be little fortresses manned twenty-four hours a day by their proud owners, living in or above the premises. Business was often slow to come by, and the luckless shop assistants were expected to work hard and long so that the proprietor could show a profit at the end of each day.

Mr Garner of Horsham told me of his first job after leaving school, working in a local shop selling boots and shoes. The opening hours were long and the young assistant was instructed to keep the display of shoes outside the shop, until the very last minute of the day, even after the pubs had turned out their patrons. When I asked whether any pairs of shoes were sold at that late hour, Mr Garner dismissed that possibility with an emphatic 'Nooh'.

From *Memories of Slaugham* by W.H. Kensett, we read of a small shop at Warninglid, kept by Mr Rayward.

A new customer of the shop asked if he should run a weekly account. 'Oh, pay as you go. Pay as you go', was the answer. He complied by dropping sixpence in the shop, and the rest in single coins all the way along the road. The luckless shopkeeper had to run after him, picking up his cash as he went.

Jury Cramp was the name above a very well-known shop in Horsham's main street. Here the Cramp family sold watches, clocks and jewellery. A huge pair of spectacles hung above the shop, as a trade sign, telling the town that the shop was also an optician's (these spectacles are now proudly displayed in the local museum). The Cramp family were well-known as strong anti-drink campaigners, in fact the original owner, old Mr Jury Cramp, ran a temperance hotel in Market Square.

With the subject of temperance in mind it was surprising that Jury Cramp's son should tell me of the vast quantities of tea which had been made for the school children at the Queen Victoria Jubilee celebrations. He said it was like tea he had never tasted before, which was not to be wondered at, as it had been made in barrels supplied by one of the local breweries.

Jury's grandson was kind enough to give me a copy of a home produced book titled *The Jolly Journal of Jury Cramp Ltd.* It is a hilarious record of life in this local shop through the years from 1872 to its closure in 1985. Most of the happenings in the book took place in the 1920s and 1930s; the record being started by the two sons of Jury Cramp – Walter and Henry Cramp.

The first entry mentions a customer who wanted his money back, after buying a pair of spectacles. He said, 'I can't read nothing now, Master. I was told if I bought spectacles I could read. I bain't no scholard – I can see letters alright, but I can't read'.

Another customer said, 'This 'ere

Not all trade signs were stationary – a 'well bread' trade vehicle in Horsham in the 1930s.

watch won't go, Master. I thinks it wants a drop of ile. I warmed her – shook her. There's a little hair in her. I pulled one end out, but t'other end is fixed in works'.

Later in the book, there is a flashback to the days of Mr Jury Cramp (c.1890). Mr Cramp is upstairs in bed with a cold, and Mr H. the shop manager has locked up at closing time. He calls upstairs, 'Good night, Mr Cramp. I'm off now. We have taken one and sixpence today. Hope you feel better'.

One more gem from this lovely book. A riddle which asks: 'Why is a Cramp like a member of parliament? The answer, because he has MP at the end of his name'.

Mr Amos Chart of Horsham (corn and coal merchant) gave the local schoolchildren rides in his cart on the day of their annual outing. Amos was known to the children as Father Chart, and at their morning prayers in school they thought it was him they were praying for when they recited 'Our Father Chart in Heaven'.

The five-wheeled pentacycle, used in Horsham in the 1880s by postmen and bakers. It was known as the Hen and Chickens.

*I*n 1982 Mr Bob Wickens, who had been born in 1899, told me about Mr Sendall, the butcher in Middle Street, Horsham, in his youth.

Mr Sendall was most definitely a local 'character' who was a trifle over-fond of his drink. Sometimes he would stand in the Carfax, looking upwards, until a small crowd gathered, and he would then walk away. Some days he might see someone he knew outside his shop, and would take it into his head to call them in, in order to give them a present. Sometimes this would be a choice cut of meat. He would occasionally take threepence or sixpence out of his till and give young Bob, who worked for him, the price of a pie from a shop in West Street, which used his own best English beef.

When he visited the pub opposite his shop, he would sometimes ask a stranger if they would like a drink. If they replied either yes, or no, all well and good. But if the answer was, 'I don't mind', then he would turn away saying, 'Neither do I'.

One day he had a sovereign, which he was quite convinced was a fake. Everyone else assured him that it was all right, but he was so sure that it was a dud that he insisted on selling it to a soldier in the pub for a shilling.

Sometimes he would leave his shop and till completely unattended when he was away drinking. Strangely enough his books were very neatly kept, in spite of the condition he might be in when he worked on them. One day he was suffering with gout in his fingers and took to his bed. When someone else tried to help him by keeping his books in order, he was very annoyed.

---

*M*any shops employed apprentices, who were invited to learn the trade, but were paid a very low wage. But not all the aggravation for the youngster came from the employer, as the rest of the established workforce were equally tough on the green employee.

The hapless lad would be sent on fool's errands, such as requests for striped paint, left-handed hammers or a yard of pump water. But it did not always work to the apprentice's disadvantage. One lad who was sent for a 'Round Square' returned from the pub with a round of drinks, telling his mates that he had brought the 'Round', but they would have to 'Square' it with the landlord.

In the printing trade the lads were subjected to a charming custom at the end of their apprenticeship, known as 'Banging Out'.

For this they might be placed in a tin bath or similar receptacle, with a beastly concoction poured over them – containing such things as ink, cat food, sawdust, custard, manure and even more unmentionable materials. To add to their misery, they were then trundled round the streets, so the townsfolk could witness their discomfort and to cap it they were expected to buy their tormentors a round of drinks at the end of it all.

In the 1930s shops were still using a form of apprenticeship for young lads of around 14, who wished to learn the trade. No doubt they did learn a great deal, much not even connected with their trade. They were also a very inexpensive form of labour, being expected to cope with everything demanded of them, from cleaning the shop to boiling milk twice a day for the coffee drunk by their senior colleagues.

One Sussex shop had a custom where the young lads had to wheel round the owner's and manager's cycles from the back entrance of the shop. They were then instructed to rest them carefully against the kerb, so that the owners could depart in style without undue delay. They had strict instructions not to 'ride' the cycles, but to wheel them carefully; but needless to say these were seldom observed.

Markets and fairs were popular places for buying things which were not normally available in the small local shops. My mother loved the cheap jack's stall in the Horsham weekly market, although she was scared of the farm beasts that occupied nearby stalls.

At the famed Horsham July Fair on the Carfax, the Fat Woman offered a bottle of wine to anyone who could span round the calf of her leg with two hands. There is no record of the prize ever being won.

Blacksmiths had a reputation for wit. Mr Kensett of Slaugham recalled Mr Burchfield of Warninglid who spent over-long in the Half Moon after work.

One evening, although it was bright moonlight, he borrowed an umbrella to take home. He was asked, 'What do you want with an umbrella on a fine night like this?' The answer was, 'Well, it's fine now, but likely there will be a storm when I get home'.

Shopkeepers' signs served as a form of advertising, just as window dislays do today.

Shoreham High Street once had a sign which read, 'Here he lives old Uncle Nat. Try his oysters fresh and fat. Full-roed herrings fit to burst. Table beer to quench your thirst'.

In Rye High Street a man who had a horse and chaise for hire, advertised it thus: 'A horse and chaise to go all ways. Whether they're good or bad. Besides I have here, I do declare. A very thoughtful lad'.

Lewes High Street once had a picture outside a barber's, of a man hanging by his long hair to a tree, whilst his donkey galloped away. The inscription went: 'Oh! Absalom, unwisely prig! Hast thou worn a periwig! For had thy luckless head been shaved, thy life most surely had been saved'.

At Hailsham a very distinctive sign said: 'Old Wenham begs to say. On every Hailsham market day. He being a licensed auctioneer. He writes and takes in orders here'. Also at Hailsham another sign read: 'As other people have a sign. I say just stop and look at mine'.

One old Sussex trade sign that still survives – this is at Arundel.

At Arundel one can still see a sign which goes back many years, although it has several times been re-worded and re-painted. 'Old Harry's nephew works here. Repairs boots and shoes and is not dear. His leather is good, his work is quick. His profits small, but he gives no tick'.

The sign as it was when Mr Spooner was at work.

S treet sellers were part of the daily life of Sussex towns and villages. In Horsham, 'Fishy Smith' sold fish and vegetables from his horse and cart. He had a cottage where he kept pigs, much to the annoyance of his neighbours.

Mrs Vincent recalled Fishy Smith's rejoinder to her request to buy a shilling's worth of fish, but no vegetables (her father had an allotment, and grew plenty for his family). Fishy barked at her, 'Buy your fish where you buy your vegetables'.

On the coast, Public Tea Gardens enjoyed a period of great popularity in the late 19th and early 20th centuries. Near Eastbourne, Mr W.J. Wootton ran the famed Wannock Gardens. He published a little book, telling patrons all about the gardens, which was written with his own singular brand of humour.

On page four we are told that 'fish stimulates the brain, but fishing stimulates the imagination'. On page ten he launches into poetry, with this gem:

'Said the old black rooster
to the little brown hen,
You haven't laid an egg
since goodness knows
when.
Said the little brown hen to
the big black rooster,
You haven't been round as
often as you uster'.

Page fifteen informs us that, 'A peach is a glorified plum, with a seal jacket on' and 'England expects every man visiting Wannock to eat Wannock Peaches'. Turn to page twenty nine and you will learn that the Tea Lawns specialise in Courtship Salad – 'Lettus alone, served with tea'. On page thirty two we leave Mr Wootton with his parting shot. 'Do have a cup of something before you go – but don't pass remarks about our coffee. You may be weak and old yourself someday'.

The Wishing Well at the famous Wannock's Tea Gardens in the 1930s.

Many places had their very own local 'characters'. Mr Newnham told me about a wonderful Henfield personality who was known as 'Shake' Gander. He worked for many years for a small building firm, run by Alf Gander (no relation to Shake). His trade was that of a humble painter and decorator journeyman, but when he died in 1990 at over eighty, he was mourned by a great many Henfield folk who remembered him as a most likeable rogue – a womaniser, over-fond of his drink, but always very generous to others, and great fun to be with.

When Shake's old cycle wore out (and the men were expected to get to their painting jobs on their own bikes), he borrowed the machine belonging to the boss, which was a much better one than his own. He continued to use it, unnoticed, for several months, until one day Alf saw it at one of the jobs. 'That looks like my old bike over there', was his surprised comment. 'Yes', Shake replied, 'And it's time you bought some new tyres for it!'

Another time, later on, when the boss had begun to fetch and carry the men in his own car, Shake and the others couldn't be seen at knocking-off time. Soon afterwards they strolled nonchalantly up the lane with their bags filled with blackberries. Judging by the quantity, it was obvious that they had spent the afternoon gathering the fruit, rather than working. When taxed with this fact, Shake denied it, but this didn't stop him demanding some of the apples from the boss's orchard, to go with the blackberries. In spite of this, and other similar escapades, Shake was treated as a valued member of the firm, more like a friend than an employee.

Drivers of country taxis have always suffered much from the peculiarities of their fares. Mrs Godsmark told me of the experiences of her father who was a Hastings taxi driver.

A regular fare was an elderly man who was very nervous. He would admonish the driver if he drove over 20 miles an hour, and he carried a hunting horn which he blew when they came to a road junction.

Mr Wootton's humour would probably have been enjoyed by the carters who once stopped off in Horsham for a night's rest at one of the local hostelries.

Mr Bernard Lintott writing in 1938 recalled how, when the carters had loads of Horsham stone from Stammerham, they would sometimes leave their carts in Market Square, stabling their horses at the Anchor Hotel nearby. One night some other carters unloaded all the stone from one cart, took off the wheels, and then built up the cart again underneath the Town Hall, which in those days was supported by arches. Next morning the carter put his horses into the shafts of the cart and loaded up, but the load would not come out through the archways. Accompanied by well-meaning advice from the bystanders, he had to unload everything and dismantle the cart in order to get it into the roadway.

Publicans should appear in this section, although I have failed to discover any humorous stories concerning them. Perhaps the profits were too small to bring a smile to their lips, or so it might appear from the story told to me by Mr F. Barton.

Mr Barton's brother worked in the windmill at Rushlake Green, near Heathfield, and one night when returning home late, he broke his clay pipe. When he called in at the local pub for his nightly pint, he had sixpence in his pocket. He bought a pint of beer for twopence; and five Woodbine cigarettes for twopence. A new pipe cost a half-penny, and matches a farthing. This still left him with one penny and a farthing change.

Coins of tiny value were treated very seriously in times past. In the 'Parsons' chapter, I related how Father Cassidy visited the nearby ironmonger's shop and paid his account in small change.

This was not the only occasion when the shop was subjected to this kind of treatment, as a well-known Fun Fair lady, Ma Benson, is also recorded as having paid a bill of seven and sixpence in silver three-penny pieces across the same counter.

Probably a complete book could be written concerning humour on the Sussex railways, but here one story must suffice. It concerns 'Old Bob', a porter at Haywards Heath, possessed of a very loud voice. (If the wind was in the right direction, his platform announcements could be heard over a mile away.)

One night Bob was moved for one shift to Three Bridges station. A group of railway workers from Haywards Heath were returning on the last train from London. They woke suddenly at Three Bridges to hear Bob's familiar tones, but were too dozy to make out the actual words. So they all tumbled out of the train, only to discover too late that they had not actually arrived at their home station.

The story about the day's takings in the shop reminds me of a similar tale of a Sussex bank, which closed at the end of the day, when it was discovered that the door had not been unlocked in the morning, although none of the staff had noticed.

To complete this section, here is one more Horsham 'character' remembered by Miss R. Reeves. The man was her grandmother's step-father, Tom, who was a local chimney sweep who lived in Park Street. He had a donkey and cart to carry his rods and brushes.

At least that was the original intention, but in the winter the donkey would be left dozing in its warm shed in Denne Road, and Tom would rise at dawn, load his gear on to a handcart, and push the load – sometimes for several miles – rather than take his beloved donkey out on an icy road. At other times he would spend hours in the shed, talking to the beast and polishing its harness. At weekends he would buy it some old ale as a treat.

If he ever forgot something, he would leave the cart where it was, telling his two dogs to watch over it, which they did very efficiently.

SAUCY SIMPLETONS

In every community there were those who were 'different', and there may have been a certain amount of friendly fun at their expense, but it seems likely that several of these local characters played up to expectations, deciding that it was more fun being an amusing person than just a dull one.

In Horsham for instance, 'Ole Dick' (Dick Fillary) appeared to enjoy making people laugh, and stories of his latest escapades must have been passed around with a good deal of glee, and have now been firmly planted into local folklore.

A typical story concerning Dick, told how when he was to meet a man at the Fox and Hounds pub on the Worthing road, he made the arrangement, 'If you get there first, you put a stone on the wall. If I get there first, I'll knock it off'. When a farmer asked Dick, 'Have you counted those sheep yet?', his reply was, 'Yep, I counted 'em all but one, but 'ee run about so much, I couldn't count of 'ee'.

Another tale told of how Dick was seen walking down Middle Street with a look of grim determination on his face, and with his arms held out firmly in front of him. 'Can't stop now, been sent to measure a door', was his explanation.

When a friend of his was given the job of cleaning out the pigs for extra pay, Dick remarked, 'T'aint fair – I can do all the dirty jobs, and yet Joe can clean the pigs out'. Another day he was heard to remark, 'There's ole Joe. He gets eighteen pence a day for night work, and I get nuffin' – that's sumthin', ain't it'.

One Sussex countryman said to his mistus, 'Tis a long time since I've took a ollerday. So next marnin' I'm a gonna lay abed till purty late'. This meant seven o'clock when he had his brekfus and went down to the village. He set hisself down on the manure heap, and sat and smoked all day long, for says he, 'Tis a long time since I took a ollerday'.

Simple Mike (Mike Hambledon) of East Sussex, was another likeable character who it appeared, charmed his public with a childish brand of innocence.

When Mike was seen selling home-made matches (bits of wood without even brimstone on them) he remarked, 'Indeed, brimstone do make 'em smell so bad'.

When someone tried out the old test of asking Mike which he would prefer, a half sovereign or a half crown, his rejoinder was, 'No, no. Mike won't be greedy – Mike will be content with the little one'. (It must be admitted that this is not the first time that this apt rejoinder has been credited to a likeable but simple character.)

On another occasion Mike walked into a barber's shop in Hastings to be shaved, but found he only had one penny rather than the two that were needed. He thereupon negotiated with the barber to shave the whiskers off just one side of his face, leaving the shop perfectly happy.

When a magistrate sent him to prison, he is said to have replied, 'Well, gentlemen, I'll goo, but I'm sure I shan't like it'.

'Short back and sides.' A Sussex barber at work during wood-cutting.

Some of these delightfully simple characters became known by interesting and descriptive names, although exactly how they had acquired them was sometimes a mystery.

Take for instance Molly Mothballs (or Old Kate), whose real name was Kate Cochrane. She walked the lanes around Fletching, with all her worldly goods in an old pram. It appeared that her name was derived from her trade of selling mothballs to the country folk.

On rare occasions, when she felt she needed it, she made her ablutions in the village pond. She would knock on cottage doors on her route, offering a can with a little tea in it, and requesting boiling water, which was never refused. Her usual costume consisted of an assortment of old clothes, worn one on top of another. During the Second World War, Kate was hit by a car, and was discovered by a villager, face down amongst the wreckage of her old pram and its contents. It was said that inside the lining of her ancient coats, they found a small fortune in notes.

Another character with a descriptive name was 'Watercress Jack' of Forest Row – presumably his name was derived from his trade, whenever he felt like following it.

Jack lived rough in an old shed, and was never known to do any real work. Like Kate he pushed his belongings around in an old pram, occasionally selling watercress and sphagnum moss. Most of the time he was a silent figure, but after a few beers he became too voluble, and the difficulty then was in shutting him up.

Most of these characters seemed happy in their simplicity. For instance, one simple man quoted by the Rev J. Coker Egerton in his delightful book *Sussex Folk and Sussex Ways* remarked, 'I've been to Lewes court six times. Three times they found me guilty, when I hadn't done nuffin', and three times they let me off when I was guilty'. So he felt that justice had been done.

Needless to say, some of these unique characters could show considerable cunning on certain occasions. A man known as Verrall of Lewes, set fire to himself in the Bear Inn and then jumped in the river. He quickly emerged lower down and ran home and changed his clothes. He then returned to the pub, and amused himself watching several men dragging the river for his body.

Brighton 1901 and the complete personnel of the Wheeler Band!

Some simple folk managed to acquire a limited fame, which has become the stuff of local history. Brighton has rejoiced in many strange characters, even into modern times.

One of these Brighton 'characters' was Henry Cope, who was known as the Green Man in the 1800s. Aged around 30, he dressed as a dandy entirely in green, even to green seals on his watch chain. He wore a huge cocked hat with gold tassels, and his carriage, gloves and wigs were all green. Although obviously a gentleman, he was always alone, and it was said that he would eat nothing but green fruit and vegetables. One day he leapt from a window of his lodgings on to South Parade, running to the edge of the cliff and then plunging to the beach below. He was carried injured to his rooms, and after this was not seen again.

Sometimes a lack of common-sense was balanced by other gifts, showing that nature can be cruel and kind at the same time.

George Watson of Buxted earned a name for his skill as a mathematician, although in other respects he was certainly below par. Described as having a gentle but half idiotic countenance, he quickly earned the nick-name of 'The Sussex Calculator'.

Born in the village in 1785, he was poorly educated and unable to read or write. But he was a genius at anything connected with figures or feats of memory. He could recall every day of his life from an early age, including the day of the month, where he was on that particular day, and what the weather was like. When these gifts were recognised he was taken on a tour of Sussex, and was then able to remember all the churches and pubs in every town and village he passed through. The Sussex historian Mark Antony Lower wrote, 'I saw him trudging up Malling Hill, near Lewes, with his battered hat chalked all over with figures, showing some mathematical feat which he had forgotten to rub out'.

George Watson. Known as the Sussex Calculator, he was brilliant at maths but hopeless at other things.

Some of the characters described in this chapter were probably veterans of the 1914–18 war, who found it difficult to fit into normal life after the terrible experiences they had endured. For instance there was Whistle Pipe Joe (Albert Newport) who during the 1920s walked the Sussex roads.

As his name implied, Joe enjoyed playing a whistle pipe and singing ribald songs, the latter much to the annoyance of his audience. But among his more endearing qualities was the habit of sharing his food from a black billy-can with his feathered friends.

Stan Parsons recalled 'Mad Jack' who came into Horsham from Barnes Green on his cycle, adorned with rabbits, hares, pheasants and partridges. As soon as he had sold his wares, he spent the cash in various pubs before setting out on his wobbly way home.

It is easy to see odd characters such as 'Mad Jack' as merely figures of fun, but perhaps we should ponder on how much their personal appearance contributed to their personalities.

'Banjo' and 'Fuller' were two odd looking men who lived at Three Bridges in the 1920s. The latter was particularly ugly with a cast in one eye, and he appeared to leer at all the little girls, who half in jest ran away screaming when he appeared. Together this strange pair pushed a handcart, piled high with all kinds of rubbish, although it was never certain whether they were intent on buying or selling. The first man played the banjo very badly, hence his nickname. They lived together for several years in an old cottage, which now lies beneath the motorway.

Faith Woods told me about a Slinfold simpleton who was often the butt of jokes by the local boys, not an unusual thing where such characters were concerned.

One day one of the local lads donned a white sheet and proceeded to claw at a box tomb in the churchyard as soon as the victim was in sight, crying out, 'Let me back in, let me back in,' as he did so. The result was not quite what he expected, as the simple one seized the sexton's spade laying close by and dealt the joker a resounding whack, saying, 'You silly B . . . You shouldn't have cum out in the fust place.'

several stories of Sussex men are concerned with their affection for the old round-frock or smock, and their reluctance to give it up in favour of more modern garb.

A country man went to London wearing his smock, and thus attired called to visit his daughter who was in domestic service. As he left the little boy of the house enquired, 'Liza, why does your Dadda come to see you wearing his nightgown?'

Arthur Beckett, the Sussex author, noted an old man in a Downland village who always attended church in a round-frock, a wide-awake hat, a pair of hedging gloves and a pair of sheepskin gaiters. A Harting man, William Shier, had a daughter who worked in the town. She was ashamed of her father's old fashioned attire, and one Sunday hid his smock. When he failed to find it in its usual place, he despaired. At the last moment she produced a fine new coat, which he donned with reluctance. Later he said, 'I were so ashamed of un, when we cum to Harting, I took un off and walked in my shirtsleeves pertending I were too 'ot'.

Because in fact the fine old smocks were something to be worn with pride, though not everyone owned one. One old man was noted for his normal garb which consisted of a mixture of old clothes held together with safety pins, bits of string, bootlaces etc. Asked if it was a lot of trouble undressing, he replied, 'Wal you see, I be done up fer the Winter'.

But then simplicity was often a cause for pride.

Many Sussex men were reluctant to give up their traditional smock.

Alf Murrell of Horsham told me about Jim Tidy, who was a local character in the early 20th century – a time when such characters were apparently quite common, and were valued for the zest they brought to daily life in an otherwise rather humdrum time.

Jim dressed in very horsey attire, and on market days could be seen riding horses bareback up and down The Bishopric. One day in a pub he had a basket with three pheasant feathers protruding from it. Someone was unwise enough to offer him five shillings for the contents. Jim accepted with alacrity, but when the cover was removed, there were just the three feathers and a basketful of potatoes. One day someone took pity on his scant wardrobe and gave him an old dress suit. But Jim said it was too grand for him, and sold it to another man for ten shillings – and he wore it happily around the town.

Another Horsham eccentric, described to me by Mary Page, was Florrie, the daughter of a porter at Horsham market, a place normally full of local 'characters'.

The market men kept Florrie supplied with tea and food, and at the end of each market day she could be seen with a huge broom 'helping' to sweep out the cattle pens, obviously with great delight, even if with little skill. There were other market characters at this time, such as 'Omo', who gained his name due to his grubby appearance.

Sometimes local characters were not completely lacking in intelligence, at least not by their own standards. Mr M. A. Lower the well known Sussex historian, told this story.

A visitor to the village enquired for Mr Pocock of Alciston. The man he spoke to replied, 'Never heered an him, an' doan know any sich pleace'. After further enquiry it turned out that the man the enquirer had been speaking to was in fact Mr Pocock himself. When this was pointed out he said, 'You should ha' axed fur Mus Palk o' Ahson.'

It seems that Sussex folk have mostly treated their simple neighbours with care and even affection. This is born out by the words on old tombstones in Sussex church-yards such as 'A harmless man', 'A poor simple old fellow' and 'A poor simple maid.'

To conclude some slightly more modern 'characters'. From a village on the Sussex-Surrey border there is the story of the local lad who took a day off to walk into Guildford to see the new fangled 'lectric light. He came back disappointed, saying that there was nuffin' to get excited about. Unfortunately he made his visit during the daytime.

In the 1980s I was told by several people of the man known as the Mayor of Shoreham, who walked between Shoreham and Worthing each day, dressed in old style clothes, suit and spats, bowing and waving to each car that passed. There were apparently similar characters in other parts of the county.

And lastly, a personal memory from the years shortly after the Second World War. In Horsham there was a character who the children called 'Venus' because he claimed to have come from another planet. His main claim to fame was that he rode around on an old cycle with a cardboard box over his head, with apertures cut for his eyes and mouth. At a Christmas 'Dickens Dinner' in a local church hall, a reader had just reached a dramatic moment in *A Christmas Carol* when there was a loud knock at the door. Upon opening it, we were greeted with the sight of Venus complete with his cardboard box. No one seemed to know what became of him after that night.

CHEERFUL CHARACTERS

In old Sussex, ladies of advanced age were often known as 'Mother . . .' or 'Grannie . . .' These terms were affectionate, rather than critical, although it was true that a certain amount of innocent humour was obtained from the sayings and doings of these ancient ladies.

My own great-grandmother, was a village nurse, and her activities and utterances lived on in the family.

When Gran tripped and fell as she entered a local store, the shopkeeper hurried forward to help her. Brushing aside his assistance, she barked at him, 'Young man – how much is your shilling a pound butter?' When a daughter asked her if she had been out for a nice doddle, she replied, 'Doddle? No. When I go out, I go for a walk'. When Lucy Broadwood of Rusper (the respected folk song collector) wrote a letter asking Gran to visit her, she remarked that 'this is someone I am likely to fall out with', although subsequently they became good friends.

From the valuable Petworth Society Magazine (June 1953) we hear of Grannie Pratt of Graffham who was a particularly useful member of the village community. One of her specialities was attending to a body before burial, and when a neighbour reported that her husband was unlikely to last the night, she is said to have replied, 'I'll come round in the morning – but if he hasn't died by nine o'clock, I can't do it, as I've got to be pig killing'.

One of the attributes of these elderley ladies was their unfailing cheerfulness, in spite of adversities.

An old crippled lady of Horsham lived in an ancient cottage in London Road. One year two local lads volunteered to wheel her in her invalid chair to the Sunday School Outing in Hurst Park. Later the same evening they met in the town, and one asked the other whether the old lady had enjoyed herself. As an afterthought, he enquired, 'Did you bring her home?' The second boy replied, 'I thought you did'. They ran to the park, and found the old lady serenely sitting in her chair surrounded by a herd of cows.

A woman of worthwhile qualities was Martha Gunn, famous in Brighton as 'The Queen of the Dippers'. These were the ladies who assisted the bathers when they braved the terrors of the sea, and Martha was a particular favourite of the Prince Regent.

Martha was well-known to the staff at the kitchens of the Royal Pavilion, and one day the Prince (who also liked to visit the kitchen area) found her there, and noted with amusement that she had secreted a large pat of butter beneath her apron. The Prince had many faults, but the lack of a sense of humour was certainly not one of them. He managed to jostle old Martha in to a position close to one of the ovens, and soon it was apparent that her girth was not entirely natural, as a pool of fat began to drip around her feet.

Martha Gunn, bathing-lady
of Brighton and a favourite
of the Prince Regent.

Many towns had their favourite 'characters'. In Arundel, Amos Stroud, known as 'Shucks' was a town favourite, working in agricultural engineering for 59 years. He was undoubtedly a 'rough diamond' but popular with most.

When Amos's boss hit his head on a beam and asked Shucks if it was bleeding, he replied, 'Bleedin'? Why, you can't get blood out of a turnip.' One day Shucks and his gang heaved a barrel of beer from a pub to their job, broached it, and ran it until all nine galloons had been drunk. But they then completed the job in record time.

A popular Horsham character in the 1930s was Mrs Nellie Laughton – a local councillor who dressed in a 'Lady Bountiful' style and was often to be seen around the town, handing out sixpences to small boys, or sugar lumps to tradesmen's horses, from a store she carried in her capacious handbag. One could say that she bubbled over with benevolence, and the townsfolk viewed her with a mixture of tolerance, affection and amusement, but often more of the latter.

Sometimes Nellie would hire a taxi, filling it with youngsters so that they could ride around the town in style.

As a JP she was known to pay a culprit's fine herself when she presided on the bench. One Empire Day she was seen behind a table erected outside her house, handing out threepenny 'Joeys' to all the school children. During the early days of the war, she almost patted me on the head when, as a teenage apprentice, I served her in a local shop, telling me that I was carrying on nobly whilst the men were at the front.

Another Horsham character of a slightly later period was Yorky (real name Thomas Hunt). He was the last of the 'outside porters', filling a need with his handcart, taking luggage from the railway station, or collecting coke from the gas works. This was obviously the reason for his earlier nickname of 'Cokey' which eventually changed to 'Yorky' due to his North Country accent.

'Yorky' knew everyone, or appeared to, and would greet all he met with a cheerful word. In 1964 he set fire to his home, a caravan in a field. He had lived there for eight years, but had been ordered to move, as the site was needed for building. After this he found lodging close to the centre of the town, but no one seems to remember when he left or died.

The next story concerns a lady of some means, who could, if she had wished, have led a life of some comfort and enjoyment.

However, old Mrs Gatford of Horsham chose to live as a recluse and she had not left her house for around twenty years before her death. Her coach had been allowed to drop to pieces, and her horses left to graze in rich pasture. In her will she left enough for bread to be provided for the poor of the town, and there was also £15 towards the well-being of her cats and dogs. Her remains were placed in the inner one of four coffins, the outer one of marble. Her funeral was held at night (one of the last of such events to take place during the hours of darkness), and she was interred in a vault in the Dissenting Meeting House.

A lady known as the Queen of the Beggars, married the 'King of the Rooks' (real name John Cole) in Horsham parish church in 1837.

The King and his Queen were driven to the ceremony in a one-horse carriage, from The Bishopric (then known as 'The Rookery' – probably due to the character of the other ladies who dwelt in this part of the town), where the bridegroom was a shoemaker. His bride kept a common lodging house, nicknamed 'The Beggars Opera'. She was known to be extemely fickle, so the townsfolk were relieved when the ceremony finally took place.

Some 19th century personalities were slightly more 'way out' than others, and these included the 'quack' doctors and self-proclaimed medicine men who travelled the Sussex countryside.

Consider 'Doctor Sequah' (real name Hannaway Rowe) who was born in 1884, became a surgeon, and then took to the Sussex roads as a herb doctor. He wore Indian chief's regalia, and went from village to village with a four-horse wagon, which carried a brass band. He was noted for massage, and also teeth pulling (the band came in useful to drown the patient's cries). One day it was said he extracted 45 teeth in less than an hour. Although he made a great deal of money, he died a pauper with few mourners.

Cheerful Characters 53

Horsham had several town criers in the 19th century, when these gentlemen were very important members of the local community – imparting news to those who had no other means of learning it.

One of the best of the Horsham Town Criers, and a great local favourite was Dan Roberts, who was well-known for his gorgeous apparel, and the size of his nose. When walking down Horsham's narrow Middle Street, it was said that he had to turn his head to allow a horse and cart to pass him.

One of Dan's drinking companions was the then Duke of Norfolk. He was a character in his own right, often remaining unrecognised when he walked around in old clothes. He was said to be fond of trains, and often frequented Arundel railway station. One day a party of Americans arrived and told him to carry their bags, and even rewarded him with a tip – which he gravely accepted.

Dan Roberts, the town crier renowned for his mighty nose.

ne of the best known Sussex eccentrics was undoubtedly Squire John Fuller of Brightling (Mad John, or Honest John, depending on one's point of view.) He was several times MP for Sussex, although it was said that he spent £50,000 getting himself elected. He loved building follies on his estate; of the six he built, Brightling Needle and Brightling Observatory are probably the best known.

Squire John could never resist a gamble, and one day he wagered with a friend that Dallington church spire could be seen from his window. Upon returning home that night, he found that he was mistaken, so in twenty-four hours he had a spire built on his land, which looked exactly like a church seen from a distance. (In those days, if you had the money, you could obtain enough workers to build almost anything in such a short space of time.)

He died aged 77 in 1834, and was laid in a tomb of pyramid shape, with (it was said) a glass of port and pack of cards to hand. Glass was supposed to have been sprinkled around him, so that the Devil would cut his hooves if he came to claim him. Squire John was larger than life, but was withal a kind man who did a tremendous amount of good in his lifetime, contributing much to the life of the villagers.

Jack Fuller's Mausoleum in Brightling churchyard. The last of his many follies.

Arundel was not the only Sussex town with an eccentric Duke. In the 17th century, the 6th Duke at Petworth (known as 'The Proud Duke') made life a little difficult for those around him.

Everyone who left the Duke's presence was expected to walk backwards until they were outside the room. His two daughters were instructed to stand beside him when he took his afternoon nap. One day, one of them felt particularly tired and decided to sit down. Her father was not as soundly asleep as she thought, and cut £20,000 out of her inheritance.

After such a 'difficult' character, it comes as a relief to hear of a famous personage with a strong sense of humour.

Sir Roland Penrose, the British surrealist artist and art collector, lived at Chiddingly. The Royal Academy decided that one of his pictures could not be included in their show, because it had a swear word in it. He agreed to repaint it, but included a pair of hands signalling the same four letter word in sign language.

The Great Omi' (who lived at Ripe in his later years) could have been an eccentric at almost any period, although he actually flourished as recently as the mid 20th century.

'The Great Omi' was a member of an elephant worshipping cult, and had his face and body covered in stripes. A former army officer, he lived in a caravan, and had his teeth sharpened to points, with elephant teeth in his ears, and a small elephant tusk in his nose. I saw him once in Brighton, and it was quite a shock.

George Belton of Madehurst who had been a champion ploughman in his youth, and was always ready with a yarn or a song, told me many good stories.

One of his tales was of his childhood days when he was sent with his brother, about two miles from home to fetch a crate of beer for a party. On the way back, they felt thirsty and tapped one of the bottles, arriving home with one bottle short. He expected to be in trouble, but the adults just laughed and said they would probably have done the same.

Sussex can lay claim to one of the most famous humorists of all time. This was Andrew Borde, sometimes known as 'Merry Andrew', who lived at Pevensey for some time in the 16th century. He claimed to be a monk, a scholar and a physician, but he evidently enjoyed a good joke.

Andrew's most famous work was a book called *Merry Tales of the Wise Men of Gotham* (there was a place of this name near Pevensey, although it is not certain that this is the Gotham he wrote about). The Gothamites were said to have drowned an eel as a punishment for eating the fish in a pond. The 'Wise Men' also kept a nightingale a prisoner because it kept them awake with its song. They placed a hedge around the tree where it perched, but were astonished when it flew away. Another story in this strange but entertaining book is of a man who saw the moon reflected in water, and thought that his horse had swallowed it. Andrew ended his days in Fleet Prison in London in 1549, where he must have found rather less to laugh about.

Pevensey seems to have had more than its fair share of odd characters. One mayor of the town was handed a letter, which he began to peruse upside-down. When the messenger timidly suggested that it would be more easily read if it was the right way up, he was told, 'Hold your tongue. While I am mayor of Pevensey, I will hold my letters whichever end upwards that I like'.

ANDREW BORDE.

Andrew Borde – the monk, writer and clown of Pevensey.

*L*en Reed wrote a lovely little book in 1988 which he titled *Slinfold – Through 80 Years* (if only more local folk would put pen to paper so charmingly).

In his book, Len tells of a local character known as 'Old Uncle Tom'. His wife, Aunt Hannah, insisted that Tom should go to church each Sunday. He would sit rather unwillingly in what was known as 'Cadger's Row', to be woken up regularly by the verger for snoring during the sermon. One Sunday he went hunting for hazel nuts instead, when he was spied by a farmer, who admonished him, 'If you were in church, you would not be stealing my nuts'. Tom's reply to this was, 'If you had gone to church, you would not have seen me'.

Another story in the book is of an old man who died, and when his sister told his pal, 'You won't see him today, as he died in the night', the reply was, 'Did he leave any 'bacca?' (This reminds me of a similar tale told to me by Mabel Bryant of Shipley, about an old lady who died, and a little girl immediately asked, 'Who had her shoes?'

One more story from the same source. Old Moke drew his weekly Old Age Pension from the post office, and immediately handed it to the publican opposite, saying, 'You might as well have it now, as you will have it all before the week's out'.

---

*I*n slightly more recent times Scan Tester (of Horsted Keynes) was a folk musician who achieved some degree of fame in the world of traditional music in his later years, becoming justly popular, both as a performer and as a personality.

I am reminded of one story which was told of Scan (or perhaps it was another elderly folk musician of a similar ilk?). The player had been booked by the organisers of a Folk Music Festival, which was taking place in a Northern town. The first concert went off well, with further events planned for the evening of the following day. The visiting musician was left to his own devices on the morning of the second day, and wandered around the strange town, eventually becoming completely lost. Coming to a railway station, he found there was a train leaving for the south, and he decided to take the line of least resistance and jump on it. The organisers of the festival were left wondering what had happened to their star guest.

On to more cheerful stories. There are many concerning old Henry Burstow of Horsham, famous in his lifetime and since, as a great folk singer, bell ringer and local character.

Henry was always anxious to add new songs to his vast repertoire, and one day he tried to persuade a carter to sing one which he wanted to learn. The man was shy, and thought that he might be laughed at for his 'Sussex burr'. So he was persuaded to sing it without an audience, but of course Burstow thought this too good to miss, and hid out of sight in the inn parlour, learning the song without difficulty.

As Henry Burstow became older, he was noted for a few small eccentricities. He had a windmill mounted on a post in his garden, which made so much noise it kept the neighbours awake at night (some said it could be heard on the Warnham Road, about a mile away). One night one of the neighbours climbed the post, and tied up the model mill, while Burstow was away bell ringing at

Warnham. When he returned he was kept awake wondering what

Henry Burstow, a Horsham character born in 1826. He brought people into church by his bell ringing but did not attend church himself.

was wrong with his mill. In the morning he found out, and took the hint, adding some washers to the model to quieten it.

Henry was something of a local celebrity, even in his own lifetime, although his views did not always fit with others. He was an agnostic, and was noted for having told the vicar, 'I fetches 'em in [speaking of his bell-ringing talents], and I leaves you to send 'em away'.

We are indebted for some reminiscences of old Sussex written by Mrs Anderson, printed originally in *The Countryman* several years ago.

Mrs Anderson was writing of an old farmer called Bridger, who brought his son to be baptised, giving 'Beelzebub' as the child's name; saying that as it was in the Bible, the clergyman was obliged to use it. Eventually he was persuaded to amend this to Augustus Caesar. The same man went to the Great Exhibition of 1851 with his wife. After a while they became separated, and his wife asked a policeman to find him. When this was done, he asked the policeman how he had found him among many thousands of people. 'Well you see, sir. You are not dressed like other people,' which was very true, as he had fiery red hair plaited in a pigtail, and tied with a white satin ribbon. Moreover he was clad in a white smock, knee breeches and gaiters.

In 1992 Mr Frank Venn told me some stories about an old Horsham couple in the early part of the 20th century, who were noted for being very tight-fisted.

Every morning the man could be seen making his way up the street carrying a white jug. His destination was not the pub, but the local butcher's shop. Here he was allowed to hang the jug beneath the carcase of a newly hung beast. When the jug became full of blood, he carried it home, and his wife mixed it with breadcrumbs and made rissoles, which lasted them the whole week.

One day a local timber yard offered its offcuts for fire lighting free of charge. Most went for the fair sized pieces, and left the dross. But our hero took a sieve, and went away with everything that would not go through.

dmund Austen contributed some amusing reminiscences of old Sussex folk to the *Sussex County Magazine* in 1942.

A rich man had become interested in the local cricket club, supporting them in various ways. Then suddenly he decided that the cricketers must play their matches on Sundays, as he had no time to watch cricket on weekdays. This the men refused to do, and the squire closed his field against them, although they eventually obtained the use of another. The furious landowner then ordered the club to return certain items which he said had been bought with his subscriptions. A collection was made which enabled them to return to him his donations. Not long afterwards the disillusioned squire sold the estate, and the village saw him no more. A perfect example of the traditional Sussex 'wunt-be-druv' attitude.

Another example was given, which involved an unpopular vicar at Udimore. Tom Neeves the village carpenter had been engaged to paint the Ten Commandments over the chancel arch in the church. When the clergyman inspected the work, he noticed that there were but eight commandments. On expostulating with Neeves, he replied, 'Ah well! I reckon there's as many up there as what you'll kip'.

Some fun at the expense of the Sussex police early in the last century.

One of my own personal memories is of a Sussex private school in the 1930s, which was run by the proprietor (and headmaster) along the lines of a large public school.

The fact that there were only around thirty pupils did not mean that the school could not have a school motto, houses dignified by colours, and a cap and gown for the master. The black gown had seen better days, and was well singed at the back where the owner had caught it in the fire when he assumed his favourite position in front of the fireplace. (The pupils who were nearest always had great fun beating out the flames with tremendous enthusiasm.) When the headmaster took the school swimming, he left them to their own devices whilst he enjoyed himself. Returning to school for the afternoon, he would announce that swimming had made him too deaf to take any lessons, so he would read to the pupils for the rest of the day – much to their delight.

Many of my memories of this strange establishment are mixed up with what may be termed school folklore – in which the master's high black cycle, and his battered black hat featured. The tales included such gems as the day he caught the wheel of his cycle in the railway track of the level crossing, and had to abandon his machine. Similar tales featured the black hat, which was supposed to have blown off as he crossed the track, to be flattened by an oncoming train. The fact that the cycle and the hat still continued to enjoy an unblemished life, in no way spoilt the enjoyment of these stories. The cycle also featured in an account of how the master rode into the nearest town, and walked back leaving his machine outside the post office. This may have happened once, but was hardly likely to have occurred as many times as the tales maintained.

When the school got into difficulties due to cash flow problems, all the school furniture disappeared, and the pupils were taught in the drawing-room of the house, sitting on armchairs or the floor. This was a prelude to the complete closure of the school, although by this time the pupil numbers had shrunk to about half the original.

A little book, *Alfriston* by Rex A. Marchant, is full of good stories. One tale is abut Mr Stephen Wood, who in 1775 agreed for a wager to walk from Alfriston to Lewes and back again (about 18 miles), in five hours. Heavy rain fell all the time, but he managed it in 4 hours and 20 minutes, after many bets had been placed on the outcome.

From the same book there is a story of a young lady who was buried in the churchyard in 1816. Following the event, one old man (admittedly a little deaf) claimed that he heard a noise from the grave. Eleven days after the original burial the grave was reopened in the presence of the minister, who was perfectly satisfied that all was in order. Another resident had such a dread of being buried alive, that he had his coffin fitted with a grating connected to another close to his gravestone.

The last of our 'Cheerful Characters' is 'Old Eb', who was recalled by a contributor to *Sussex Life* in 1968.

The old man was trudging up a hill with a sack of potatoes on his back, and gratefully accepted the offer of a lift. It was noticed that he kept the sack on his back. He turned down the suggestion that he should place it on the floor of the cart, on the grounds that 'this way it do make it easier for the little pony'.

Another classic tale concerned the day when he was digging up his potatoes. A passer-by asked, 'Ow be they turning up, then?' To which he replied, 'Biggest and best be small and bad, and even the little 'uns bain't no size whatsomever!'

FOLK and FAIRY TALES

If we wish to explain what constitutes Sussex folk humour, then the easiest way is to give some examples. For instance if a Sussex speaker is asked, 'Do people die here often?', the immediate reply will be, 'No, only once.' An expression of surprise might be, 'Well, I'd rather see a church fall down.' And what more definite description can there be than, 'So drunk, he couldn't see through a ladder'? Sometimes a local reference helps to make a point, such as, 'This must be Cuckfield – there's houses on both sides of the street.'

To move on to something less general, let us consider Sussex mud and the place it has played in Sussex humour through the years. It is considered a particularly rich and viscous substance, far superior to anything that other counties can produce.

Sussex mud. Still as sticky as ever, even in the 1950s (the author is the one struggling). (Photo – Cecil Cramp)

This is from a letter sent to Queen Anne in 1895, concerning a journey on the Crawley Road. 'We set out at that time by torchlight, and did not get out of our coaches, save only when we were overturned or stuck fast in the mud. His Highness's coach would have suffered very often if the nimble boors of Sussex had not frequently supported it with their shoulders.'

One of the best known Sussex mud stories relates how a man noticed a hat on the muddy roadway. On lifting it, he was amazed to find a human head beneath it. He enquired after the health of the owner, commenting that he must be finding his situation rather uncomfortable. The reply was, 'Not nearly as uncomfortable as the man whose shoulders I'm standing on, or the horse that he is riding.' This story has been told, and retold many times, with all sorts of variations.

Sussex story-tellers are never short of a subject, when the county's mud is mentioned. For instance, Sussex women, and animals, have always been credited with extra long legs, due to the effort of walking through this particularly glutinous substance.

There are a number of local stories which include references to Treacle Mines. Many villages rejoice in the possession of one of these mythical mines, leaving youngsters puzzled when their elders speak of such things with a perfectly straight face.

One of the best known Treacle Mines is supposed to be at Sompting, and some of its stories are told by Worthing author Alfred Longley in his book *Alexandra Terrace*, in which he tells of an imaginary character 'Jimmy Smuggles' who works at the mine.

Another village which is noted for its own humorous tales is Piddinghoe. In this village the natives are said to indulge in such strange antics as shoeing their magpies, hanging their fields out to dry and digging for moonshine. All these weird occupations can be easily explained. The magpies are the black and white Sussex oxen; chalk is ground up in water and spread on the fields to dry. And smugglers hid their smuggled spirits in the water, to be retrieved at a later date.

ne would perhaps expect to find the fairy folk included in this chapter on folk humour, but in fact they have always appeared to be sadly lacking in any real sense of fun. The dialect version of Fairies emerges as Pharisees, and to some this seemed to be a good argument for the actual existence 'as they are mentioned in the Bible'.

One Sussex fairy story which broke away from the general rule, concerned two thieves who stole a pig, which they secreted in a sack. Unknowingly they placed the sack over a fairy's hole. One of the little folk released the pig, and put himself in the sack instead. As the thieves climbed the hill, they heard, 'Dick, Dick, where are you?' And another little voice replied, 'In a sack, pick-a-back, riding up Beeding Hill'. A slightly similar tale was told about a family who were tormented by a troublesome imp. To get away from him they decided to move, and loaded all their possessions on a cart. As they left, they were discomforted to hear a little voice from the middle of the cart, telling all those around that he was looking forward to living in his new home.

The fairies dance on Midsummer Eve at Chanctonbury Ring.

ne of the nicest examples of supernatural humour occurs in the ballad *The Farmer's Cursed Wife*, well known in Sussex as *The Sussex Whistling Song*, on account of its whistling refrain. Leaving aside the 'Diddy-fol-days', these are the words:

There was an old farmer in Sussex did dwell,
And he had an old wife, as many knew well.

Then Satan he came up to the man at the plough,
'It's one of your family that I must have now.'

Now Satan he got the old wife on his back,
And he lugged her along like a pedlar's pack.

Oh, then she did kick all the young imps about,
Says one to the other, 'Let's try turn her out.'

She knocked old Satan against the wall.
'Let's try turn her out, or she'll murder us all.'

Now he's bundled her up on his back again,
And to her old husband, he's took her again.

'I've been a tormentor the whole of my life,
But I ne'er was tormented till I took your wife.'

Much magical humour appears in the old Mumming Plays, performed in Sussex at Christmastime by the Tipteerers. Here is the Doctor in the West Wittering Play:

> 'I can cure the hipsy, pipsy, palsey and the gout.
> A strain within and a strain without.
> If I break his neck I will set it again,
> I won't charge you one single farthing for my pain.'

From the Compton play, the Doctor again:

> 'I had a man brought to me the other day; indeed, he was not brought to me, he was wheeled to me in a left-handed wheel-barrow. He could not see anything without opening his eyes, and could not speak without moving his tongue.'

These plays are full of crude but effective lines such as these, with the nonsense stored up in the character's minds from year to year. In fact the non-sensical words are considered almost as important to the play, as the basic story.

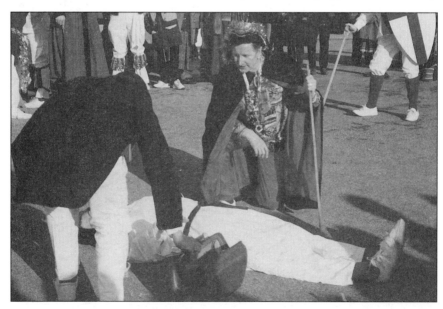

Traditional Sussex Mummers Plays still survive. This was at Sompting on Boxing Day 1993, with the 'Doctor' attending to his patient.

robably the best known Sussex 'tall tale' concerns the Mare's Egg. (It must first be admitted that some other counties also claim this story as their own.)

Two Londoners visited a certain Sussex village, and spotted a local with a large pumpkin under his arm. When they unwisely asked him what he was carrying, his reply was, ''Tis a mare's egg'. The visitors asked if they could buy it, and a bargain was struck, but as they carried it away in triumph, the one holding the 'egg' tripped and dropped it, causing it to roll down the hill. It stopped near a bush, frightening a hare which ran off. The men ran in pursuit, believing that their mare's egg had hatched, and shouting, 'Stop our colt! Stop our colt!'

Many jokes belong particularly to certain villages. A tale from Rottingdean set the locals chuckling, in spite of its grim sequel.

A thief made off with a sheep one night, tying it to a boulder on the cliff top whilst he went for a drink. Later he returned, fell asleep beside the sheep, and during the night the animal got the rope twisted around itself and the boulder – at the same time throttling the thief. The boulder is known as the Hangman's Stone, and to prove the truth of the story, may still be seen to this day.

The Hanging Stone at Rottingdean.

Some local jokes had a supernatural twist, which undoubtedly made them all the more popular with the listeners.

One youngster agreed for a wager to spend a night in a supposedly haunted church. As none of his mates would accompany him, he agreed to drive a six inch nail into the floor of the church, to prove where he had spent the night. In the morning, his mates found him expired in the place they had left him, with the nail driven through the edge of his smock and into the floor.

Much less worrying are stories such as the one from Ditchling, where a post was erected to commemorate the murder by Jacob Harris of Richard Miles in 1734. Some time after the event the men from the local inn bet one of their number that he would not spend a night close to Jacob's Post on the Common.

When the nervous hero took up his lonely vigil, he decided to try some conversation to help his courage. 'Hello Jacob, how are you tonight?' was his opening gambit. From the other side of the post came the reply, 'Very wet and cold.' Our man turned and ran, and did not stop until he was safely within the bar parlour among his friends. The joke was eventually explained to him, but somehow he failed to appreciate the humour of it. The genuineness of this story sadly has to be doubted, as I have been told an almost identical version, but this time concerning a murder near Burpham in 1771, where a post was erected on the site of Jack Upperton's Gibbet.

Jacob's Post – not the place for a lone vigil!

A t Henfield it is still possible to see the Cat House, which below the eaves displays a marvellous collection of black cats forever playing with canaries in their paws.

For the origin of this unusual decoration we must go back to the 19th century, when the house was the home of a Sussex eccentric, Bob Ward. Nearby lived Canon Woodard, famous as the founder of the Woodard Schools. For a reason unknown, these two were at loggerheads with each other, and no opportunity was lost to score points off one or the other. Things came to a head when a canary owned by Ward, was killed by the Canon's cat.

Ward was determined that such an outrage should not be forgotten, so he fixed black effigies of the cat around the house, rattling them by means of a string whenever the man of the cloth passed by. He also arranged a jingling collection of scallop shells on wires to add to the annoyance, and he even resorted to firing a number of toy cannons in his garden. To add to all this he hung flags from trees, and blew a ram's horn whenever his enemy hove in sight. This story may have become exaggerated by time, in fact it has even been suggested that the whole thing was invented by a journalist. But there is

Cats galore at Henfield. (Photo: Ivan Stevens)

no doubt about the effigies of the black cats, or that Bob Ward was a genuine local eccentric. Obviously the modern cats are reproductions, kept there to puzzle tourists and keep this bit of fun alive.

Another form of house decoration – a Herstmonceux
sign fashioned by creepers a hundred years ago.

 ow for something much more light-hearted. Here is my mother's account of how the colours worn by a bride were likely to affect her married life.

Married in Black – you will wish yourself back.
Married in Blue – love will be true.
Married in Brown – you will live in the town.
Married in Yellow – ashamed of the fellow.
Married in Green – not fit to be seen.
Married in Pink – you will live at the sink.
Married in Red – you will wish you were dead.
Married in Purple – you will look simply awful.
Married in Grey – you will live right away.
Married in Mauve – you will look like a toad.
Married in White – you will look just about right.

An old custom which still survives, is that of St Valentine's Day on February 14th. In my mother's memory this was an important day for all the young ladies.

The first person of the opposite sex seen by a young lady in the morning, would be considered their Valentine for the coming year. The obvious thing to do was to hide from those you did not wish to see, or to get a friend to blindfold you and lead you to the man of your choice.

A children's rhyme was, 'Good Morrow, Valentine. For 'tis yours, then 'tis mine. Please to give me a Valentine.' Knocking on doors and reciting the above, was supposed to bring forth a reward of money, fruit or cakes – the latter known as Valentine Buns.

On St Valentine's Eve one could make sure of a suitable future husband, by fixing a bay leaf on the corner of one's pillow, then in the morning, taking the yolk out of an egg, filling the centre with salt and eating the whole thing – shell and all, without drinking or speaking afterwards.

In 1886 a Sussex post office appealed to the public to post early for St Valentine's Day, such was the amount of additional mail expected. A local paper commented, 'It is to be hoped that we have seen pretty well the last of St Valentine's Day and the silly practice of this wholesale distribution of meaningless trash.'

At certain places in East Sussex it has long been the custom to scramble for hot pennies on certain days of the year.

On Mayoring Day in May at Rye, after the election, the new Mayor threw hot pennies from the upper floor of the Town Hall. Apparently it was originally the fishermen who scrambled for the coins, but in more recent times it has been the local children. One theory is that the Mayor when he was also the MP for Rye, was actually bribing the townsfolk to vote for him. Another story has it that when Rye had its own mint, and pennies ran short, sackfuls of new pennies hot from the mint were distributed in this manner. At Hastings it was apples, nuts and oranges which were thrown from upper windows, for the fishermen and boys to catch.

To end this section, here is a Sussex story that begins rather like an orthodox folk tale (or even an urban legend), but ends very differently. It was sent to me in 1996 by John Fry, who had heard it several times from a Worthing scout master in the 1960s.

An odd egg-shaped object is purchased at a jumble sale. This is placed on the mantelpiece where it incubates in the heat of the fire. Upon opening, a birdlike animal emerges, and is dubbed a 'Rarey'; and what is more it learns to speak. However, it has an enormous appetite, and eats its owner out of house and home. The latter tries smothering it, and poisoning it, but all to no avail. Finally he takes the Rarey to Beachy Head (to show it the view!), and steps backwards for a run up to push it off the cliff. The Rarery understands what is happening, and spies the waves below. Looking reproachfully at its owner it says, 'That is a long way to tip a Rarey.'

The hapless paupers in the dreaded workhouses were allowed a little cheer at Christmastime. This is how one newspaper in 1881 ended its Christmas Day report: 'The old women had their usual allowance of snuff, and the men enjoyed the soothing pipe over the fire with the customary glass of porter – indeed a happier family it would be impossible to conceive.'

OLD GEORGE and the CHRISTMAS CONCERT

In 1995/6 the *West Sussex Gazette* published a series of humorous stories featuring a Sussex character called Old George, set in the fictional village of Brigley in the 1920s. This was the first one, and it is republished by permission of the *Gazette*.

I have my own seat in the corner by the window in The Grapes. Most of the regulars have their own particular spots and visitors are not popular if they try to pinch them. I particularly like my seat, as it gives me a good view of almost everything that happens in the pub.

Opposite to me is an armchair which is considered Old George's own special seat. Mind you, it wasn't always his. It seems only a few years ago, when it was his dad's – and he was also known as Old George. Then the first Old George died, and somehow his son, Young George took it over, and before long he became Old George. Like his Dad, he's never had a praper trade. Somehow he gets by with a doing other folk's odd jobs, helped out it's said by a little bit of poaching. (In his Dad's time, it was smuggling, but we won't go into that.)

Almost as much a fixture as George himself is Bit, his old dog, who is usually asleep beneath his chair – so quiet and peaceful-like that you wouldn't know he was there, that is unless you tread on his tail or something, and then all hell breaks loose. Like George, Bit has hidden depths.

Most evenings the talk will be pretty general, but every now and then a current topic will take everyone's fancy. A few weeks ago it was the annual Christmas concert which the old vicar had asked John English, his clerk and sexton, to get up in the parish 'all, and which this year was to be in aid of the church roof. Why this should worry the old boys in The Grapes, is a bit of a licker, as hardly any o' them ever set foot in the church, except p'raps three times in their lives.

But the subject kept cropping up, as it seemed that the old vicar just couldn't find anyone to provide a big attraction. All the regular turns 'ad bin booked, of course. Truth to tell, he would have been hard to put to keep 'em away. But if the hall was to be full, then there just 'ad to be somethin' a little bit unusual-like. By the week before the concert it seemed that the vicar and John English were at their wit's end to provide anyone special. Then as often happens at times like this, it was Old George who came to the rescue. He upped and said, 'What about a conjuror?'

Now very few of the boys present knew 'xactly what a conjuror was, but they didn't let on like. Even those who did know what he were talking about, had no idea how to get hold of one – but it seemed that George had an old friend from Chichester way, who knew a man who knew a professional conjuror. After a good deal of talk, in which serious doubts were cast upon George's ability to arrange anything as complicated as booking the services of an artist for a concert, it was agreed that he should go ahead. Of course this was because by this time nobody had any better ideas.

A few days after this, Old George in his usual 'told you so' kind of voice, announced that everything had been fixed, and that the conjuror would appear, always providing he were top of the bill. Nobody objected to this, as all the locals liked to get their own acts over and done with early on, so they could set back and enjoy picking 'oles in the rest of the concert.

Sure enough on the night, the hall was full, no doubt mainly because of the unknown artist who had agreed to honour the little village of Brigley with his presence. As in previous events of this sort, old John English were the Master of Ceremonies, and he announced the first act, which was Saul Champion, the village miller, with his recitation of *Christmas Day in the Workhouse*. He started off alright, but at about the 30th verse when the audience were becoming a trifle restive, he stopped to adjust his 'spactacles' and in so doing, dropped his script. The audience took this as a suitable moment to applaud vigorously, and the MC seeing his chance, stepped forward and thanked Saul for his contribution, and the young lads in charge of the curtains pulled them across with a flourish.

The next item was Miss Eleanor Twippet, who played the piano. This wasn't too bad, excepting that she only knew one piece, *The Robin's Return*, which the village lads at the back of the hall, tried to whistle, rather unsuccessfully. Her performance was by no means helped by the piano, which resolutely refused to utter a sound when middle C was played – but then everyone was used to that.

There was then an unexpected interval, when all the lights went out, and backstage whispers were heard to the effect of, 'Who's got a shilling?'

The lighting having been reinstated, the concert was able to proceed. There were then two short items: first Willie Benstead and his musical spoons (this was announced as a medley of Christmas carols, but no one recognised any of them). After this Dicky Pratt, the village constable, attempted to sing *The Miner's Dream of Home*. This was hindered rather than helped by Miss Twippet on the piano, which by now had added several more non-playing notes to its repertoire.

The first half concluded with a solo cornet rendering of *The Mistletoe Bough* by the vicar himself, which would have been alright if he hadn't had to stop every few minutes to gather up his wind, as it were.

The curtains, which had been borrowed for the occasion from the new winter stock at Miss Gimpson's emporium, were drawn for the interval and the local lads transferred themselves outside, while their elders and betters discussed the entertainment so far, and of course the treat still to come.

Up till then, no one had so much as seen a glimpse of the conjuror, although the vicar assured everyone that he had arrived, and was getting his-self ready in the dressing room (which was really the cleaner's room, at the back of the hall).

Sure enough when the curtains were drawn back for the start of the second half, there he was in a rather worn looking black suit, and a top hat and cane, which he told us was his magic wand. Most were a bit disappointed like, as they had expected something a bit out of the ordinary; and he was a very ordinary looking tibster of a man; the sort you might pass in the street any day without realising that he was a famous conjuror.

He began with a few tricks utilising a long piece of string. After a bit he got so tangled up with it, that he threw it away in disgust. Unfortunately Miss Twippet was standing in the wings, and it hit her across the face. She gave a shruck thinking she was being attacked and swooned into the arms of the curate who was behind her. She appeared quite satisfied with the situation, but the curate turned a rather startling shade of red.

Then the conjuror called for a volunteer from the audience, and Mrs Shaggs volunteered her young Jimmy, son of Old Jimmy 'Bacca' Shaggs, who was one of the regulars at The Grapes. The conjuror proceeded to root around in young

Jimmy's shock of hair, bringing out such things as eggs an' coins (although he must have been the first person ever to have got any money out of a member of the Shaggs family). After a while he seemed to lose interest in this, and asked for a cloth to wipe his hands. Then he cut up a lot of coloured ribbons, and straight away made them reappear uncut, which would have been quite good if the bits of cut-up ribbon hadn't reappeared beneath the table, when young Jimmy trod on the edge of the tablecloth and pulled it off, as he was leaving the stage.

He then announced his climax, which was to make a number of articles mysteriously fly across the hall, from his hat on the stage, to a closed box at the back of the hall. For this trick he asked the audience to provide articles, and Old George started things off by offering his Dad's gold watch and chain. Not to be outdone, other folk followed with various odds and end of tie pins, necklaces, other watches and jewellery.

Placing all these in his tall hat on the table, he tapped it several times with his wand, and announced that in five minutes all the treasures would be magically transferred into the box at the back of the hall. Then he sort of faded away, and everyone started looking at their watches – at least them as still had them to look at, and counting off the minutes. When the time was up, the MC lifted up the lid of the box with a flourish, and showed it to be – completely empty. He then checked the tall hat on the stage, but of course that were empty too. Now this wasn't exactly what the audience had wanted to see, and to a man (and woman) they charged out of the hall looking for the conjuror, but it seemed he had done one more disappearing trick, and was no wheres to be seen.

Of course, all this caused no end of bad feeling in The Grapes during the weeks that followed, mostly aimed at Old George (in fact the Christmas spirit seemed to be completely lacking in The Grapes by that time). But George protested his innocence, pointing out that he had been the first to offer his Dad's watch and chain.

It was about three months after this, when things had simmered down a bit, that Old George appeared one evening wearing a watch and chain very similar to the one he (and his dad) had always worn. Of course, everyone demanded to know where he had got it, and he calmly pointed out that he was wearing his old Dad's second best watch, which had allus been kept in a drawer upstairs.

He even showed them a scratch on the back of the watch, which he said was not on the best one. Somehow nobody seemed to believe him, but they didn't know how to prove otherwise.

AND SOME
OF THE REST

One of the difficulties in writing a book of this sort is that there is a problem in knowing when to stop. As one story follows another, so yet more tales spring to mind, just asking to be told. But every good thing must have an end, so here is a whole collection of 'ends' to bring the book to a conclusion.

Sussex pubs often have good stories associated with them – stories which are relished by the regular patrons, who are usually ready to pass them on to visitors, with perhaps occasional embellishments.

The strangely named Bax Castle at Two Mile Ash, near Southwater, has had several reasons put forward for the origin of the title. One which crops up from time to time is that the hostelry was so called after the famous composer of the same name, who lived in the area. It was even said that Sir Arnold Bax supplied the inn with whisky during the war. However it would seem that all these tales are completely untrue. A little more likely is the story that the building was named after a weaver named Bax who lived

close by, and who owned a donkey, which he was in the habit of tethering in front of the inn. During a spell of very severe weather, the unfortunate beast froze to death one night, and in the morning some of the regulars stood it up against the wall, where it stayed for some time. This was said to be the origin of the local expression, 'Going down to the Donkey', or just to the 'Donk'.

The lovely old inn, The Swan at Fittleworth, beloved of fishermen and artists, had its own archway across the road.

One day a local farmer Jim Rapley promised his workers a gallon of ale if they could pile hay high enough on his cart, to touch the arch. But nobody seems to know if they actually succeeded.

Many interesting stories exist concerning Alf Shrubb of Slinfold, who many considered the world's greatest runner.

The story-tellers have it that Alf started his sporting career at 30 by racing with a trotting horse over a five mile course. The race was watched by over 1,000 people (some say it was 2,000). The horse won, but by only two minutes. Later he ran to a fire at Christ's Hospital, passing the fire engine on the way. There were many tales concerning his legendary capabilites as a runner, and one lady told me how her father and Alf both ran to reach a fire at Brighton – but of course Alf got there first.

The runner Alf Shrubb
with some of his trophies.

Over the years I have been very lucky in having come across so many Sussex folk with good stories to tell. Ethel Powell who was brought up in Portslade had a fund of great memories, which she was only too pleased to share with me.

One of Ethel's tales concerned her uncle who had a grand voice and who led the choir in church. However, his memory for words was less good than his singing skills, so he invariably sang '. . . and him and her . . . and she and him . . . and him and her' instead of the proper words; although none of the congregation appeared to notice.

Her father cut his arm very badly one day, and the wound became infected. He grumbled and groaned so much about it on the Sunday morning, that her mother who was cooking the dinner, grabbed one of the hot potatoes and slapped it on the wound. Her dad danced around the kitchen, but mother hung on and would not let him remove it. Next day the wound began to heal.

However, it was her grandfather who had the grandest sense of humour in the whole family. One day his pony strayed, and was found wandering in the lane eating the grass on the verges. A neighbour took grandad to court, and the magistrate fined him five shillings. The old man thanked him, and remarked, 'I thought I would at least be hung – and I never could abide anything tight around my neck.' The court was not amused, and the fine was increased to ten shillings for his 'contempt'; but grandfather thought it was worth it.

The late Gordon Hall had an apparently inexhaustible fund of good stories, most of them with some degree of humour in them.

Typical of these was his account of the old Horsham gaol being demolished, when some of the ironwork was used in the construction of a bridge over the Ouse. Later the bridge was itself blown up, but too many explosives were used, and some of the metal was blown into the river. Gordon had the unenviable task of swimming out and attaching ropes to this material in order to drag it to the bank. As Gordon said, it was just as if the old ironwork refused to give up, and the whole job was a disaster from start to finish – although years afterwards he could see the humour of the whole episode.

Two Sussex lads decided they would like to have a day out in their school holidays, and go by train to Littlehampton. This was the first time they had been allowed to embark on a trip of this sort by themselves, so having received their parents' permission, they agreed to be very well behaved.

Arriving at the old-fashioned railway station they set out for the river and the beach. Halfway there one of them spotted a fishing line and hook in a toy shop, and decided he would like to try his hand at angling. When they reached the river they sat on the tiny pier to eat their sandwiches, and the one with the fishing line used a piece of his bread as a bait. Throwing it down into the water he awaited results, but without much hope.

Imagine the surprise of both of them (and several bystanders) when there was a great flurry of activity in the water, and it was soon evident that a large fish had been hooked. This was quite beyond the experience of the two lads, but with help from many willing hands, the catch was landed and an expert soon had it detached from the tiny hook and line. Several experienced anglers looked enviously at the catch, and during the rest of the day the boys were stopped several times with a request that they would show the fish, which the lucky one was carrying in his satchel.

At the end of a wonderful day, they caught the train home, and eventually exhibited the catch to astonished parents. Curiously enough the mother and father of the boy who had caught the fish, kept the local fish and chip shop!

There are several good stories from my own memory, of a Sussex country dance band which flourished for a quarter of a century. During most of that time, the pianist was a lovely character called Ernest, who lived by himself in a cottage, and was picked up each week to play with the band.

Ernest was not a good solo performer. In fact, I only remember him playing one rather plaintive tune from time to time – but as a band pianist he was superb, keeping perfect time and supplying just the kind of steady accompaniment needed by the other instruments. He had a way with pianos. This was just as well, as the pianos encountered in village halls and barns were of very mixed quality.

Ernest's first task before the dance started was to take the piano to pieces and almost rebuild it, but some pianos were too bad for even his ministrations. One particular example even provided a nest of mice, when the front was removed. Ernest enjoyed the refreshment interval, when he would stock up his supply of food for the coming week, eating very little at the actual dance. Sometimes he would decide to have a snooze during the interval, lying down on the bare floor well out of the way of other folk.

When the lights failed halfway

Ernest. He was known to take a piano to pieces before he would attempt to play it.

through a village dance, the band was informed that the electricity meter needed a shilling to put the lights back on again. However, the meter was high up on the stage, so that Ernest who was the tallest, had to climb on a table to reach it, and restore power.

Once he was faced with a fine organ, rather than the normal mediocre piano. Unfortunately it was locked, and the hall secretary was unwilling to allow it to be unlocked. Ernest pleaded, and assured the man that he was a skilled organist who had taken many organ exams. At last he was allowed to have the key, and he gaily played the organ with the band for the rest of the evening. It was only later that he admitted that the only organ exam he had ever taken, he had failed.

When it came time for Ernest to retire, the band faced a real disaster, and the loss of the company of a very fine Sussex Eccentric, and a perfect gentleman.

Jack Russell Lambert, who was born at Crowborough in 1898, was considered to be the smallest man who ever lived in Sussex. He was perfectly formed, but was a mere 2ft 10in tall (shorter in fact than the famous Tom Thumb).

He was always pleased to tell of how in 1917 he received his calling-up papers. He went to Eastbourne to be medically examined, and came away with a military discharge paper, to prove that he had served his country for just one day. Apparently he was a smoker of cigarettes, although there is no evidence that these stunted his growth!

Town criers have almost as many stories about them as farmers, and probably a whole book could be written about them.

Once at Brighton, a crier gave out the following announcement. 'A Holland smock, a pair of silk stockings and a gold ring, will be given as a prize to be run for by females on the sands.' Many turned up to try their luck, but it seems the whole thing was an elaborate hoax, and no contestant gained even a pair of silk stockings, not to mention a gold ring.

tan Parsons was a fellow townsman, who was so popular that he became known as 'Mr Horsham'. He always enjoyed a good story, and could be relied on to produce a few special ones from his own memory.

One of Stan's many stories concerned his boyhood when he and his cousin used a disused vault in the parish churchyard as their own private 'den'. They discovered it by climbing the iron fence around the tomb, whereupon they saw a flat stone with an iron ring in the centre. When they pulled this, the whole stone came up and steps were revealed leading to a tunnel, which in turn led to a vaulted chamber. No human remains, but clean and dry.

They used it for some time as a hideaway, taking food down with them. One night they heard the stone being moved, and then footsteps approached. Luckily their visitor turned out to be a local man who knew them, so their secret was safe.

Many years later Stan was walking with his dog in the churchyard, and decided to try and rediscover the old tomb. He was challenged by a young curate, who said rather haughtily, 'There are no vaults under this church', although undoubtedly Stan knew differently.

Apparently Stan and his pal were not the first to find their way there. An old

Horsham churchyard, where
Stan Parsons had his 'den'.

Horsham Guide of 1905 speaks of a period ten years earlier, when local boys made use of a vault below the church for a 'free and easy club'. At this time the congregation were alarmed by curious noises during services, for which 'ghosts and the unquiet dead' were blamed.

Now Stan and his stories are no more, although residents (and visitors) to the town can still remember him when they make use of a new 'twitten' or passageway in the centre of the town, which is officially named Stan's Way.

That grand old man of Sussex, Basil Evershed has always been good for a chuckle or two.

He told me the story of a new and rather dim youngster employed at Baynards station on the old Horsham to Guildford steam line. The Station Master in spelling out his duties said, 'I will shout Baynards Station as the train stops. You must do the same at the other end'. When the train came in the lad shouted out, 'Same this end.'

This reminds me of a rather similar story concerning Rudgwick station on the same line. It was here that the solitary porter would shout out Rudgwick when opposite the First Class carriages, but would change this to the dialect 'Rigick' when he got to the Third Class compartments.

Another of Basil Evershed's stories concerned his father who was assured by a very frightened lady that a 'huge snake' had threatened her on the road as she returned home. Dad went to investigate and found an old cycle inner-tube lying twisted in the roadway. Whether Dad told the lady of her mistake is not recorded, but more than likely he took credit for a gallant rescue.

Also from Basil, is the story of a Billingshurst man who suffered the sad loss of his beloved wife. On her gravestone he had inscribed, 'My light has now gone out'. When he later remarried, a local wag remarked that he should add, 'But I soon struck another match'.

There are many stories concerning the goings-on each Bonfire Night (November 5th) in Sussex.

One lady told me of how her grandfather in Lewes dressed up each year as a devil, with pins stuck in his tail, so that the folk who tried to pull it were well and truly pricked.

Although Lewes was notorious for its 5th November activities, other places in Sussex also had their moments. The *West Sussex Gazette* of 12th November 1863 carried an impassioned letter from a reader, concerning the boys living in the vicinity of a country house close to the South Downs. On the 5th, the occupants of the house were visited at 8am by seven small boys with paper caps on their heads, brandishing cows' horns. After reciting their bonfire hymn, they blew a flourish on their horns and then had to be driven away by force. An hour later, three big boys arrived dressed in the same manner and with blackened faces, and repeated the performance. They also had a 'guy' with them, which they planted before the door,

5th November at Crawley in 1914 – Bonfire Night produced many stories over the years.

invoking curses on the occupants. This sort of thing continued throughout the morning, and after a brief lull, was taken up again in the evening. The correspondent ended with the pious hope that the 'plough boys and yokels may soon learn that nearly all England has given up such mummery'.

Helena Hall told the story of how an elderly man urged the boys to 'pile 'em on' as heavy bundles of faggots were thrown on the flames of a huge 5th November fire. Not until the following day did he discover that the faggots were his own property, brought round from the back of the house whilst he cheered them on at the front.

At Rye, Bonfire Night was considered a very appropriate time for practical jokes. Once, they put a man up to his neck in a tar barrel, and barrels filled with burning tar were rolled down Conduit Hill.

The late Mr H.R. Goatcher, market gardener of Washington, told me of a Bonfire Night which he remembered from his youth in East Preston. The one local policeman had been drafted to Littlehampton to help deal with the goings-on there, and with East Preston unguarded by the law, the local lads decided to roll their tar barrels up the road to start a bonfire in front of Preston Cottage. At the crossroads they gathered all the burnable material they could find, including pea and bean sticks from the local policeman's allotment. One lady brought out a cradle saying she had no further use for it. The result was a tremendous fire, which was still burning the next morning, to such an extent that the local carters had a problem getting their horses round the corner on their way to work.

Effigies were once very popular as a means of showing disapproval of people, or of holding up to ridicule others who had stepped over the line of acceptable behaviour.

General Booth (the leader of the once unpopular Salvation Army) and the Boer War leader Paul Kruger were typical examples. As well as Bonfire Night, Shrovetide was noted as a time for making effigies, and these were then either burned or pelted with stones. In modern times at Guestling, an effigy of a publican who committed suicide in the stables of the White Hart in 1888, was a century later used to attract coins which were devoted to local charities.

ometimes toll gates were burnt as part of the 5th November jollifications, showing just how unpopular such things were. However, in spite of the hatred engendered by tolls, they often featured in Sussex stories, many of a humorous kind.

Clergy were allowed through without payment of a toll, if they could prove that they were on the way to conduct a service. One particular cleric tried to drive through without paying, although he clearly had a young lady sitting beside him. He explained airily that she was his sister. The keeper was adamant and demanded a fee for her. The matter was only resolved when the young lady agreed to descend and walk through the gate, employing the same ruse on the return journey.

A memory of the Findon toll gate tells of a man dashing to fetch a doctor to his wife who was expecting her first child. He refused to waste time paying the toll and jumped the gate; probably not the only time when horses were made to jump the hated edifice. Another way to save money was to take the horses out of the shafts, paying a toll for a single animal, and then drawing the cart through afterwards.

Picts Hill Gate in 1885 was kept by Mrs Jane Hill, who was expert at defeating attempts to evade payment. As well as her own gate,

Bicycling fun – a bicycle made for two on Brighton seafront.

she was also responsible for another at Bines Hill, eight miles away, which was kept by her blind husband. When she knew that a driver who had a reputation for evading payment was heading for the second gate, she was known to catch a train to Partridge Green station, and to be ready at the Bines Green gate to confront the astonished driver.

Horsham's last surviving toll gate was at the Star Inn, Crawley Road, Roffey. This was the gate which was supposed to be responsible for bad weather in the town. 'Leaving the Swan Gate open' was always given as the reason for strong winds across the Carfax.

Built for speed – a bicycle made for six early in the 1900s.

Much more permanent were the Follies which exist all around the county, often the cause of much speculation as to their original usage.

A typical folly is Racton Monument. This was built in 1770 by the 2nd Earl of Halifax at a cost of £10,000 and at the time was known as a 'gazebo'. Another folly, which sadly no longer exists, was Holmbush Tower, Colgate, which was 106 feet high. It was built by Thomas Broadwood in 1855–7. The man who actually did the work was a Mr Sumner, assisted by his son and another man. Stone came from the estate, and the tower had 144 steps, which were once happily climbed by visitors who were rewarded with a glass of lemonade upon payment of threepence.

Here is a small snippet of modern folklore, which concerns a vessel which ran aground on the stormy night of 21st/22nd January 1980, on Brighton beach, east of the Palace Pier.

Locals and visitors flocked to see the stricken ship, all striving to leave their initials on the side. A riddle current in Brighton schools at the time asked, 'Why did the *Athina B* come to Brighton?' The answer was, 'To get to Ship Street' (a street not far away). The vessel was towed away on 17th February, and the excitement subsided.

Toasts when drinking have always been very popular in Sussex, many of them full of merriment. Here are just a few.

> Here's to the bee that stung Adam, and set the whole world a-jogging.

> B for Bacca, and B for Beer. The Devil take those who won't come here.

> Here's to the man who eats enough to sink a barge, and drinks enough to float it again.

A reminder of old Sussex full of good cheer, although it wasn't always like that. Consider this rhyme which would have applied to some of the living-in conditions of the farm lads:

> Pork and cabbage all the year
> Mouldy bread and sour beer.
> Rusty bacon, stinking cheese.
> A chaff bed just full of fleas.

A few years ago I was sent an epitaph, written by an elderly gentleman in Lancing when he was about to give up smoking.

There lies our Fred who collected old pipes,
Fine figured meerschaum of all different types.
His ambition was plain; his tastes were few,
To colour them all an ebony hue.
Now the registrar's shadow has darkened his day.
Both Fred and his pipes are compounded of clay.

To end on an appropriate note, here are a few Sussex epitaphs with a touch of humour. Mind you, I cannot vouch for the genuineness of all of them!

Here lies the carcase of a wretched sinner.
Doomed to be roasted for the Devil's Dinner.

Here lies the body of Edward Hide.
We laid him here because he died.
We had rather, it had been his father.
If it had been his sister, we should have missed her.
But since 'tis Honest Ned, no more shall be said.

Here lies the mother of children seven,
Three on earth and four in Heaven.
The four in Heaven, preferring rather
To die with Mother, than live with Father.

He tasted of life's bitter cup,
Refused to drink the potion up,
But turned his little head aside,
Disgusted with the taste, and died.

BIBLIOGRAPHY

Austen, Edmund; *Brede*, 1946.

Beckett, Arthur; *The Spirit of the Downs*, 1909; *The Wonderful Weald*, 1911; *Adventures of a Quiet Man*, 1933.

Boys Ellman, Edward; *Recollections of a Sussex Parson*, 1912.

Burstow, Henry; *Reminiscences of Horsham*, 1911.

Doel, Geoff and Fran; *Mumming, Howling and Hoodening*, 1992.

Egerton, Rev. John Coker; *Sussex Folk and Sussex Ways*, 1892.

Ely, B.D; *Thakeham Parish Church*, 1979.

Gundry, Doris; *Midhurst Yesterday and Today*, 1984.

Kendall, S.C. (Ed); *The Sussex County Book*, 1938.

Kensett, V.H; *Memories of Slaugham*, 1929.

Longley, Alfred; *Alexandra Terrace*, 1960.

Lower, Mark Anthony; *Contributions to Literature*, 1854.

Macdermott, K.H; *Sussex Church Music in the Past*, 1922.

Marchant, Rex A; *Alfriston*, nd.

Martin, Edward; *Life in a Sussex Windmill*, 1921.

Parish, Rev. W.D; *A Dictionary of the Sussex Dialect*, expanded by Helena Hall, 1957.

Reed, Len; *Slinfold Through 80 Years*, 1988.

Simpson, Jacqueline; *The Folklore of Sussex*, 1973.